CONTEMPORARY AUSTRALIAN MONOLOGUES

for Men

Edited by Emma Rose Smith
and Claire Grady

First published in 2017
by Currency Press Pty Ltd,
PO Box 2287, Strawberry Hills, NSW, 2012, Australia
enquiries@currency.com.au
www.currency.com.au

Reprinted 2022

Cataloguing-in-Publication data for this title is available from the National Library of Australia website: www.nla.gov.au.

Cover design Alissa Dinallo for Currency Press.
Internal design by Emma Vine for Currency Press.
Typeset by Emma Rose Smith for Currency Press.
Printed by Fineline Print + Copy Services, Revesby, NSW.

CONTENTS

FOREWORD

At Currency HQ, we love Australian plays and we welcome any opportunity to talk about them. Thankfully, so do our customers and we get a lot of calls from them asking for suggestions. One of the most common requests we receive is a recommendation for a monologue. We get so many, in fact, that we decided to collect our favourite contemporary monologues into a single package—and here it is.

The selection process has been great fun, though not without moments of heartbreak. Some difficult choices needed to be made and some favourites got dropped in our attempt to get the balance right. We've aimed for diversity in writing style, age of character and length. I hope we've got something here for everyone, whatever your age and whether you're preparing your monologue for drama school, a showreel, or an audition for a professional production.

In the following pages you'll find soldiers, German rabbit breeders, bushrangers, Bollywood producers and body doubles. There's Richard Frankland and Ruben Guthrie and Nikolai Ivanov. There's a young spook spying on the South Bendigo branch of the Communist party, and an old man (and a young one) falling in love. There are political thrillers and satires and comedies and love stories and tragedies. The commonality is that they are all written by Australian playwrights and they were all published post 2000. And they are all beautifully written.

The monologues are presented here in order of length. Dean Carey suggests in the Australian audition bible, *The Actor's Audition Manual*, that the ideal length for a monologue is between one-and-a-half to three minutes. The majority of monologues included here fall within that criteria. We have included some longer monologues—these are for students completing the individual performance for the end-of-school exams. Several of them can also be cut to suit your needs so I'd recommend that even if you are looking for a shorter monologue, take a look at the monologues towards the end of the book.

We have included a brief introduction to each piece to provide context to the monologues. These include the age of the character (wherever possible), along with notes about when and where the piece is set. These introductions, however, are intended as a starting point, and are not a substitute for reading the plays themselves. A paragraph cannot do justice to the nuances and subtleties of each of the characters that appear in these pages, who are further developed during the course of the plays in which they appear. We'd also recommend researching as much as possible on the world of the play to provide further context and depth to your performance. It's also important to note that we have slightly adapted some of the monologues, cutting other characters' lines, asides or directions that don't make sense without the context of the entire play. We have added a note to the monologue's introduction to show where this has happened.

When choosing your monologue, we recommend that you pick one that you feel an emotional connection to. This doesn't necessarily mean that you should only be choosing characters that share your own personal experience, but remember that to make the monologue work, you will need to find the emotional trigger. Be culturally sensitive. Choose wisely and trust your instincts.

And so, without further ado, here they are. We hope you enjoy the following monologues as much as we have enjoyed putting the book together.

Claire Grady, 2017

TIM

From *Holding the Man*
by Tommy Murphy
adapted from the book by Timothy Conigrave

Tim is Timothy Conigrave, the author of the memoir on which this play is based. The memoir (and play) document the fifteen-year relationship of Tim and John Caleo. It's a beautiful, heart-wrenching love story. This scene appears as the epilogue to the play, following John's death from AIDS at the age of 32. Tim died just two years later.

Dear John,

I am sitting in the garden at the back of my hotel, surrounded by orange trees and bougainvilleas. After the madness of the northern cities, the island of Lipari is paradise.

I visited the island of Salina yesterday, the island where your grandparents were born. It was a bit like a private pilgrimage. It is almost barren, lots of rock and caper bushes. The café is only open for an hour and you can understand why they emigrated.

The most unnerving thing: here on Lipari there is a beautiful boy who works in the bar in our hotel. He is so like you he could easily be one of your brothers. He was born here but his family is not Caleo. He is so gentle and so shy. We try to talk but he speaks Liparota, a dialect I can't understand. He occupies my dreams: I fall in love so easily these days.

Life is pretty good at the moment: I have my health and seem to be doing most of the things I want to do before I die. I guess the hardest thing is having so much love for you and it somehow not being returned. I develop crushes all the time but that is just misdirected need for you. You are a hole in my life, a black hole.

Anything I place there cannot be returned.

I miss you terribly. *Ci vedremo lassù, angelo.*

OATES

From *Do Not Go Gentle...*

by Patricia Cornelius

Oates is in his 80s. He is nearing the end of his days and grappling to come to terms with the death of his son, Peter, who died by suicide. Their relationship had not been easy and Oates yearns for his son's forgiveness as he nears death himself. Regret is at the core of the following monologue.

That's not my forte, I'm afraid, talk between men. I've never known what to say. I like the idea of it, I like it a great deal. Like father and son talks, I like the idea of them, I thought that would be a good thing to do, to meander about, perhaps in a shed, putting something together, building something, a fence maybe, or a brick wall. Where you've got your eyes on the task, none of this intense eye-to-eye I'm talking to you, just doing your business and you chat, on and off, you chat and there's silence and you say functional things, too, like hand me the glue, or the hammer, or hold this bit of wire, would you? And things get said, about bits that might be worrying you, like something someone has said, or the amount of work you've got hanging over your head. And you might say something about what you like, and what you don't like. You might reveal things to each other and things might be said that puts whatever is niggling at you in a different light. Suddenly it might seem trivial and silly and nothing at all to worry about. But like I said, I never got into the swing of talking. My father had no skill at it, I can tell you. And me, I guess I never learnt to do it, either. I wish I could have learned. I dearly wish I could.

TALBOT

From *Myth, Propaganda and Disaster in Nazi Germany and Contemporary America* by Stephen Sewell

Talbot is an Australian academic teaching in New York post 9/11. His beliefs are at odds with the political thinking of the time. He finds himself in a Kafka-esque nightmare when he is approached by a nameless Man. In the following scene, which appears towards the end of the play, he is in a cell, being interrogated and beaten. He has lost nearly everything and is about to lose his life. This is his last, defiant speech.

If it is my privilege to be a witness and champion of Reason, then so be it, though the whole world knows how little I deserve such an honour. For while Reason has stood and guided us in the right direction, I have cowardly averted my eyes, pretending not to see what all in their secret hearts know to be true: that we live in a world of brutal injustice dying as we speak in its own stinking poison; that whole nations have been raped, robbed and thrown into slavery so we few can enjoy the pleasures we indulge ourselves with; that for all our pretence at honour, grace and beauty we are broken, crippled monsters plundering the earth; and while Reason points ever clearly the path to justice and survival, I have joined the throng leaping to destruction for fear—For fear of what? For fear of you?! For fear of you mental dwarves with your sticks and your burning crosses and your hate! For fear of you morons quoting literature without understanding it, pawing art without feeling it, breathing air without smelling it; for fear of you and your guns and your madness and your tantrums, for fear of you and what you may do as you were doing it! But Reason still stands unsullied, and Reason will be there in a thousand years' time when this new Dark Age will itself be no more than a footnote in history, and on that day, I will have a name, even if it's only the name of victim, but You. Will. Have. No. Name. At. All!

CHARLIE

From *Jasper Jones*
Adapted by Kate Mulvany
from the novel by Craig Silvey

Set in 1965 in a small town in Corrigan, a small town in Western Australia, Jasper Jones *is a coming-of-age story. This is taken from the first scene of the play. Charlie Bucktin is a bookish but brave 14-year-old. In this scene, he is addressing the audience. His innocence is quickly established in the scene below, as is the tone for the play—it's funny but there are plenty of dark secrets hidden in the town, as Charlie discovers. We have edited this scene slightly to create the monologue.*

Jasper Jones has come to my window!

He knows my name! Wow! [*To Jasper*] What are you doing here?

It's really late, Jasper. My parents might wake up—

[*To the audience*] Jasper Jones needs *me?!*

You have to understand, I've never snuck out before. I'm a virgin to this kind of thing. Actually, I'm pretty much a virgin to *every* kind of thing. Except books. So me sneaking out with Jasper Jones, who is known throughout Corrigan as the worst kid in town, well, it's fair to say this is particularly out of character for me.

In this town, Jasper is the first to be blamed for everything. Whatever the misdemeanour—nicking lollies from the store, throwing lit matches down the mines, or sneaking through fences to push over cows—no matter how clear their own child is guilty, parents ask immediately, 'Were you with that motherless half-caste Jasper Jones?'

And the kids always nod, because Jasper's involvement instantly absolves them. Their parents think their poor little child has somehow been momentarily led astray. And so the case is closed with just one simple instruction, 'Stay away from Jasper Jones'.

So me being here, under a full moon, being led by Jasper Jones past the brown lawns and gardens of my sleeping neighbourhood, past the cricket pitch, past the railway, past the power station, over the bridge, through the farm district, and knowing what my mother would do if she found out where I was ... Well, let's just say this is something *way* more adventurous than anything Huckleberry Finn ever did.

RICHARD

From *Walking into the Bigness*
by Richard Frankland

Richard Frankland is a strong and proud Gunditjmara man and Walking into the Bigness *is his story, from his work at the abattoirs when he was a teenager to his time as a field officer for the Royal Commission into Aboriginal Deaths in Custody. Through each of the scenes, his love of family shines through. The scene below is called Touch the Stars. This monologue is intended for an Australian Indigenous performer.*

I remember my pop as a man with a glint in his eye and a joke on his lips.

I used to sit with Granddad—Old Chris Saunders—cooking eels that we'd caught. His hands were huge. His back was straight and I thought that Pop Saunders was so tall he could touch the very stars themselves.

We caught those eels with his old mate Ray. Ray drives us out in his car to Darlots Creek. Pop wades into the water and, using a bobbin—a bobbin is worms threaded onto a line—and then when you got a mob of worms, you put a couple of snails in the middle and wrap all those worms around it, then, you tease the eel with it. The eel is a greedy fella, he takes a good gulp of that bobbin, and then once he takes hold, you flip him up onto the creek bank.

When they hit the creek bank Old Ray whacks 'em with a stick and puts 'em in the hessian bag. I fall asleep watching those two: splash, whack, splash, whack. I wake up and the car's rocking and we're chugging along a track heading back into town. I was only little then. My dad had died and Pop filled the gap for a bit.

I remember walking down the street with Pop; whitefellas would call him Mr Saunders. He would wave at them as they drove past in their cars, he would doff his hat to the ladies. He had a straight back, and to me he was so tall and strong I used to think he could shape clouds or pluck an eagle from the sky.

Seemed like everyone knew him, everyone liked him, whitefellas calling my granddad 'Mr Saunders'.

MITCH

From *True Minds*

by Joanna Murray-Smith

True Minds *is an old-fashioned rom com and Mitch is 32 and the wicked, gorgeous ex-boyfriend of Daisy. Benedict, who Mitch is ostensibly addressing, is Daisy's fiancé. (Benedict is described in the character list as handsome, expensive and dull.) This speech, though, is really for Daisy. It's Mitch's final pitch to win her back and he needs to inject every ounce of charm and sincerity into it.*

Let me make this simple for you, my friend. When you walked in here tonight you knew that Daisy was the most remarkable girl on Planet Earth. I could see it in your face.

And that day when you looked up—Well, there in a corner of the elevator was a girl that made every other girl pale into insignificance. And when she opened her mouth, the tone of her voice—it seemed like a really great cabernet mainlining into your heart. And when she said the word 'facetious', you thought to yourself: Here's someone with a vocabulary that's going to keep me interested tomorrow and the day after that and the day after that and all the days stretching ahead of me. And at the polar bear line, you thought: Can you believe a girl that looks and sounds that good, could be seriously brainy as well—what are the odds on that? And then when she asked you for a drink, you stood stock still and you thought to yourself: Well, this very minute, as I stand here, is proof positive that despite all the bad things that have ever happened to me, from my middle name on, I have an angel looking down on me, shining a light on me, because *I am the luckiest bastard in the universe.* Cast your mind back,

Benedict, to a short while ago when you burst through that door, a bunch of daisies in your hand. You thought to yourself, as you took in the sight of her, not: *There's the prettiest girl in the world*, or *There's the cleverest young writer of her generation*, or *There's that honey that sets my nerve endings on fire*… No. No, you looked at her [*looking at Daisy*] and you thought: *There's* [*beat*] *My* [*beat*] *Life*.

YADAKA

From *The Drover's Wife*

by Leah Purcell

The Drover's Wife *is a postcolonial and feminist reimagining of Henry Lawson's short story and Yadaka is its hero. He is between 38 and 45. In this scene, he is talking to the drover's wife. They are on an isolated farm in the Snowy Mountains and Yadaka is on the run from the police for a murder he didn't commit. In the previous scene he has helped deliver her stillborn child but despite this intimacy, the drover's wife doesn't yet know whether she can trust him. She is holding a gun while he tells her his story. We have cut the drover's wife's lines to create this monologue. This monologue is intended for an Australian Indigenous performer.*

I'm not from here. I was adopted in. North. I'm heading home. Tryin' to. I was left in Melbourne.

I ran away with a circus. South African circus, 'Fillis Circus'. I was good with the horses and bears. They did their show, startin' in my homeland of the Guugu Yimithirr, rainforest and coloured sand country, missus. All the way down the coast. I calmed a bear in rough seas. I was good with the children that came to watch.

I was with the circus for, two years. They left me then, des … des-tit—

That was my first arrest. Destitute.

In prison, dead for; cold, no clothes and a man of God, Father Matthews, helped me.

Got me out, clothed me, gave me a white name, I don't use it.

He took me to a mission, west … taught me to read, write and play the tuba.

But bein' there, listenin' to Father Matthews' stories about his God wasn't gettin' me closer to my homeland though.

I went then. Slipped away into the shadows, missus. Went on my own walkabout.

Followin' the range; The Great Dividin'. It goes right up into my homelands in Queensland.

Takin' the mountain range, I ran into other mobs, see.

I came to the Snowy Mountains with them for the big Bogong moth, Uriarra … to eat and … dance and …

Then one night I saw this beautiful woman … her skin oiled with the Bogong moth fat, shining like a full moon … and when she danced … smooth like shallow runnin' water over river rocks …

I had to be adopted to be right skin for her. To join with her. So, I was adopted into the Ngambri Walgalu. Settled in with them.

I'm Yadaka of the Guugu Yimithirr, adopted Ngambri Walgalu.

MARK

From *Caress / Ache*

by Suzie Miller

Mark is a surgeon who can no longer bear to touch the living after losing an infant during surgery. In this scene he is calling a sex line, desperate for human connection, but there is nothing sexual about his call. Though he may initially sound professional or impersonal, it should quickly become apparent that there is a deep grief not far beneath the surface.

Hello.
Um, I'm Doctor—
Mark, just call me Mark.
I've never called anywhere like this before.
No, no please don't, I don't want—
Look, I just wanted to talk to you.
Just ask you some—
I mean if you don't mind.
Can you do something for me? Please.

The person on the other end tries sexual talk.

No no, no, nothing like that.
Did you know that when someone touches you, say… your forearm— /

Not heard, but the other person says, 'forearm?'

Yes your forearm. If you run your fingertips down your forearm.
Yes, yes that's right, can you do that for me?

Did you know that while you are doing that, that there are hundreds of synapses firing in your brain, registering all the messages coming directly from receptor cells beneath your skin?

Can you do it again, just with the softest fingertips? Run them over your forearm and under your wrist.

No not to me, to yourself.

Can you feel the veins and arteries, can you feel them pulsing?

Can you touch your own arm just with your fingertips and tell me—

Tell me what it feels like?

—

Makes you shiver, yes? And?

Does it feel warm?

—

Can you, can you just hold onto your forearm for me please?

Yes like that, hold the flesh of it.

Wrap your hand and fingers around the skin, the muscle, the tissue, like you're not going to let go.

Don't cause any pain though.

Is it causing pain?

Good.

Can you tell me what it feels like?

Yes, that's right, all those receptor cells, but I don't mean that.

I mean, can you tell me how you actually feel?

You know, what feeling you get when you are held like that?

—

And do you—? Sorry what was your name?

—

Chantal.

When you have that feeling, the one you said feels alive, feels warm,

is it—

Is it beautiful?

IVANOV

From *Ivanov*
by Anton Chekhov
adapted by Eamon Flack

Nikolai Ivanov is in his late 30s and things aren't going so well for him—he is living unhappily on a farm and is in debt to his neighbours. His wife, Anna, is dying and in the scene below he is talking to her doctor, Lvov. Lvov is there to explain Anna's illness to Ivanov but all Ivanov wants is a diagnosis for his own malaise. He is, by his own admission, irritable, bad-tempered and petty. He is aware that his behaviour is appalling.

But where is the beginning? I can put my finger on two or three beginnings, but they go so far back we'd be walking and talking until tomorrow morning. You see?

He stops.

But Anna is incredible. She's amazing. Do you know—? Her parents are very wealthy? and very religious? and she gave it all up, mostly, sometimes she still prays, but she gave it all up for me? and left her country to come here? and we got married and her parents—they'll have nothing to do with her? Right? And what did I put on the table? Half this lousy farm. That no-one wants to buy. That I inherited with my cousin. Who is an idiot. And blew his half on a dud racehorse. I let him stay because his mum was kind. Where was I? Anna. She loves it here— [*wags a finger at Lvov*] remember that!—but her parents had so much money and she left them knowing they'd never give her a cent... See: where's the beginning? I don't know. This is such a long, ridiculous story...

He takes a deep breath.

I married Anna for love. We were very, very much in love. And I swore to love her for the rest of my life, but five years have passed... and somehow or other she still loves me but— [*Throws up his hands.*] And now you're telling me, very clearly, and I know it's very difficult for you to do, you're telling me that, what, my wife is probably going to die quite soon? Yah? But. But. I feel—no love, no pity. Just. Emptiness. A kind of... depleted... uninterested... sort of... indolent... I'd rather read a book than talk to you about... my wife's... fate. Anyone's fate. I don't care. [*He leads Lvov off.*] And to you, to anyone who is not me, this is probably, I would imagine, appalling. I don't understand it myself. And yet I don't care.

SNOW

From *A Town Named War Boy*
by Ross Mueller

Inspired by the State Library of New South Wales' collection of World War I diaries and letters, A Town Named War Boy *explores the impact of war upon soldiers and their families. Snow is a young Australian soldier who had his right hand shot away at Gallipoli. The following monologue is set in the immediate aftermath of battle.*

Dawn. The roll is called and how heartbreaking it is—name after name is called; the reply a deep silence which is felt, despite the noise of the incessant crackling of rifles and screaming of shrapnel.

Silence.

There are few of us left to answer to our names—just a thin line of weary, ashen-faced men; behind us a mass of silent forms—they have been with me here for some days, I have not had the time to bury them. Listen!

Silence.

Nothing there—

I am tumbling all to pieces.

He stands alone signalling with only his left hand.

Heliopolis. Palace Hospital. After the ceaseless thunder of guns, the agony, filth and desolation of the battlefield, it is like heaven to be tucked between clean sheets in the silence of this ward—the sisters gliding noiselessly about, the eastern architecture and decoration. I half expect to find myself wafted away on a magic carpet. Days fly into months—and here I am still in bed, and told that tonight I was discovered in one of the corridors in my delirium, imagining myself signalling.

Pause.

Somebody is leaving chocolates every other day. There is one patient who, in his delirium, is singing a series of convict songs, which is driving me mad, though to the other patients in the ward this causes considerable amusement.

Pause.

Here, as elsewhere, Death stalks—comrades pass out within a few hours of each other. One by one, they pass into the infinite. Leaving behind a name that shall ever ring glorious. As I look into the distant future when the sound of guns is but an echo I see the spirits of these my comrades in a boat with me—on water—we are searching for a noise—a sound—a voice in the darkness—friends who have handed to future generations a deeper meaning of the word—sacrifice.

He stops signalling.

BRIAN

From *This Year's Ashes*

by Jane Bodie

Brian is in his early 60s and has been dead for two years. He has been visiting his daughter Ellen for some time but in the monologue below, it's the first time they acknowledge the painful truth of the situation. When a full stop is omitted in the text below, it means that Brian has changed thought or tack mid-dialogue.

I didn't leave, Ellen.

I died.

Beat.

I died.

My heart stopped, Ellen. It stopped beating, for too long, kiddo. And I

I died, Els.

He moves to touch her.

I took a couple of breaths. I remember that, one normal and then one slightly bigger

But something wasn't right. Because by then my brain was trying its best to pump blood through my lungs, pump it, for dear life, throughout the rest of my body. I felt a bit dizzy, nothing to write home about. They say you feel pain, you're supposed to. Left arm for some reason, and then your chest, like a weight. That's what they say. But I didn't. I didn't even really know it was happening, until

Which is probably something. No time to really think about it, to know what's coming next. Because that, that would be a terrifying thought.

No, all I thought, I remember thinking this as I opened the fridge, to get some cool water. Best thing I ever bought, that fridge with the chiller. It was a stinking night, hadn't cooled down, not even at two a.m., air like, soup. Your mother was dead to the world, snoring, like an angel.

I opened the fridge and I thought, hang on a minute, what's that, that feeling. Because, I've given up smoking, I've given up full-fat cheese. I even said I'll sign up for the that yoga at the funny church your mum likes, that's if Maureen doesn't fucking come, in her onesie and I've just bought my first three-man tent, for when the rain stops, so what's this? What, is, this?

Beat.

There was another breath then, in between that thought, that moment and the next one. The next thought, I thought I was going to have. And God, I wanted one, a breath. I wanted to fill up my lungs, breathe it in, air. Life. So much.

Life.

By then my brain had been deprived of oxygen for too long. It was probably only ten or twenty seconds, at the most, but that's too long. The brain starts to die then, and that's when you cease to breathe, and then, well it's over then. And you. You die.

Beat.

I died, Ellen.

He reaches out to touch her and then remembers that he cannot. They sit in silence for a moment.

LON

From *Wonderlands*

by Katherine Thomson

Lon is in his 40s or 50s. He is a farmer who runs his property, Ambertrue. His daughter, Tessie, is engaged to be married to Tom. She has gone to the city for the last fitting of her wedding dress and not come back. Cathy is Lon's wife. Lon is popping a heart pill as he talks on the phone to his sister.

Sandra. Sandra. Of course I'm not saying you know where she is. You're her aunt, that's all and… I just thought on the off chance that she'd headed off to the bright lights of Brisbane on some sort of personal hens night, I don't know. I don't know what's going on inside her head.

Pause.

She went to Toowoomba for a fitting for her wedding dress and she's been gone a fortnight.

Pause.

Of course I've phoned the police, but there's not a lot they can do. Then yesterday we get this envelope in Tessie's writing. From Tessie. A blank postcard from the youth hostel where she was staying, along with a piece of black material. Dress material. Black. Cathy had asked her when she arrived to send us a sample of the fabric. Of this dress I'm meant to be paying for. That's what she sends. Black.

Pause.

It's got nothing to do with Tom, she loves Tom. Worships Tom. But she's not herself, not by a long shot. So if you get any funny calls from Tessie…

Pause.

Cathy's mother? Yes, she did. You're right. She did. Cathy's mother went very odd. And she wasn't all that old. That's true. Christ.

Pause.

What? What's that supposed to mean, punishment? You said we were being punished—what exactly do you mean?

Pause.

Here we go, here we go. You're as mad as a two-bob watch Sandra, never mind anyone else. You want to run this dried-up, windswept shit of a property you come up and do it. If it's worried you all these years, we'll leave the gate open, walk on in. Listen to me, and this is the last time I say this. When Dad died either you bought me out or I bought you out. Not a property around here where siblings didn't have to walk off. You agreed to my offer. It's why you're sitting in your little unit. And yes it is worth more now, but so are my teeth—to me—and if it's any consolation it'll be worth fuck-all if I drop dead in my tracks and/or if Tessie doesn't do the right thing and marry Tom who does know how to run cattle among his other assets. This is history, Sandra, history. Bit of advice. Lugging history on your back's a sure-fire way to become a pain in the neck.

Pause.

I hope to see you at the wedding, Sandra. I sincerely hope.

TOM

From Seventeen

by Matthew Whittet

All the characters in this play are in their teens but are played by actors in their 70s. It's the last day of school and friends have gathered in the park for a party. They are all on the cusp of great change. Tom, here, is speaking to his friend Sue. He doesn't know how she feels about him and is incredibly, beautifully, vulnerable.

I had this one the other night. It was a crazy dream. I don't know about you, but ever since we started our exams they've gone crazy.

But there was one that I can't stop thinking about.

Beat.

I was old. In my dream I woke one morning and I'd become old. It was like my entire life had passed by in the space of one night and I didn't know what had happened to it. Where it went. I wasn't scared. I wasn't even fazed. It was just how things were. It was just a fact.

I called out to my parents. But they weren't around anymore. They hadn't been for ages. And I wanted to cry. So I did. I felt like I cried for years, for all the time they'd been gone, and because I never got to say goodbye. And then that finished. And I was okay. It was like I'd cried all the sadness out of my body.

So I walked around this house, and I had no idea where I was. And I saw pictures on the wall. Of kids. Little kids. Three-, four-year-olds. And I thought… 'Do I have kids? Are these my kids?' And then it hit me. They weren't my kids… they were my grandkids.

And I felt so happy… it was like I was going to burst.

And then someone called out my name.

Someone upstairs.

So I went up.

I went into the bedroom and there, sitting on the end of the bed… was you.

You weren't young anymore. And I could see on your face that you had no idea what was happening either. You were just like me.

And we sat there. And we put a blanket around our shoulders, and tried to talk about what had happened. But we couldn't. We couldn't find the words.

So we just sat.

We both knew everything would be okay. We weren't scared at all.

And I loved you so much.

I was deeply in love with you.

I am.

Pause. He takes the letter from her hands.

The next day I found this.

Pause.

I was never going to say a word. To you or anyone. I was going to lock it all away and never think about it again… but I can't.

And when you looked at me before… when I was singing… I knew that if I didn't say something now I'd regret it for the rest of my life.

ALEX

From *The Berry Man*

by Patricia Cornelius

Alex is in his 60s. He is a Vietnam veteran who is suffering from Post Traumatic Stress Disorder. He has arrived, unexpected and uninvited, at another veteran's farm, and his motivation for tracking down his old war buddy is unclear. We subsequently learn that he was excited to go to war and by the prospect of becoming a man, but was ravaged by the effects and still haunted by it. The monologue below is the first time we gain insight into what he has suffered.

When I came home I expected to be a hero, to be an Anzac like my father and grandfather. I expected to be feted, to be clapped on the back, to be congratulated. I met a woman I'd known since I was a kid in the street and she spat in my face.

The RSL clubs told me I was a disgrace. I felt frightened and confused and lonely for a former life and returned to an Australia that disowned me.

When I came home I looked at the letters I'd sent my mum. Every page was covered in kisses. We were boys when we went and we came home swearing, drinking, whoring men. I caught up with friends and their hair was long and they'd been overseas travelling with girlfriends. They weren't grown-up. They weren't men and I was angry with them. I'd had something stolen from me and nobody wanted to report it. Nobody wanted to talk about where I'd been, what I'd done, how I'd fared; they wanted to pretend I'd never gone anywhere.

When we came home we were snuck in, split up and sent off. They said, that's it, piss off, go live a nice suburban life. For two years we'd been together, walking in each other's footsteps, signalling with our eyes, covering each other's moves, lying in bed at night hearing each other cry. We had no idea how to contact each other or whether we'd ever see each other again. We were scattered bits and I had to put us together again.

I came home to a girl who I'd written hundreds of letters. I'd held onto her in the dark, stifling nights. I'd held onto her in the mud and the slime. I'd held her hand when I walked through the maze of rubber trees and distorted light, where every shadow was someone about to take my life. I came home with pictures of our wedding already taken, our honeymoon already imagined. I knew her body, its shape, every dip and curve of her. I came home and she'd moved on. Gone.

We learned that what you are now and will be until you're dead is a Vietnam War vet. That two years of our life crawled in and took up all the room. Nothing before and nothing after fit in.

ANIL

From *Lighten Up*
by Nicholas Brown and Sam McCool

Anil (full name Anil Dixit the Third) is an Indian film director in Australia. In the following, he is shooting a Bollywood blockbuster: Bindhi Beach: Bollywood to Bondi. *John is an Anglo-Indian Australian with brown skin, who would much prefer to have white skin and not be identified as Indian.*

K*ya bakwas hai?* I don't have time for this. Kanti, cut the continuity, let's continue the shoot. Aunty! The koala. Why is he sleeping? We don't pay him to sleep. Wake him up! Bunty—the kangaroo? He's jumping, he's supposed to hop. Hoppity-hop! ... teach him the difference. Surdeep, what do you mean you can't swim!? I couldn't care less, strap on the shark fin and get back in the water. You're supposed to be a Great White, not a wussy Wobbygong. And no floaties, you know my policy—No H and S! You're not in Kerala anymore! Hey Preeti—are these the bikini babes? Ooh not them—we need pale girls with skin like a jellyfish not a bloody orange. Manoj, something's missing. Where's Ashok? Go fetch Ashok from his trailer. And wake him gently, you must get Ashok, not him. Quickly everyone the light is fading. Sunny, standby with the fake sun. Ooh Ashok! You look so dark and roasted! I told you to slip, slop, slap and beware of the Bondi sun! Make up! Wake up! Baby powder for Ashok's face. Think guys think! Put on some zinc! Ok places. Quiet on set.

Beat.

Music. Take two. Life savers, go! Lift him. Higher, higher. Hold that move. Keep lifting. Lift him higher. *Arrey Ashok*—go son go. Dancers, pop your pelvises, pop, pop, pop. And flow to the water. Side-step the sand castle. Pop your pelvises, keep on popping. Hold him. Surdeep—keep your head in the water! Hold the shark fin in position. Speedo boys speed up or Surdeep will catch you. Jump the blue bottle—careful with Ashok. Hold him! Hold him!

Ashok falls.

Aunty! Bunty! Kanti! Oh my Gods! Ashok! You dropped him you *mutha chodes*! Ashok. Are you ok my friend? Have you broken your patella? Oh my gods. *Arrey bap re bap!* Manoj?! How will we manage? Uncle! His ankle! Patel's broken his ankle uncle, and his patella. He cannot finish the film. My Bollywood classic just turned into a Greek tragedy!! Uncle, call an ambulance. Tell them Ashok Patel has broken his patella! Ashok, how can we ever replace you? It's such a shock. Aunty. Bunty. Kanti. *Vaat* ve'll do?

Anil sees John.

Oh my gods. Is it my lucky day? Have the clouds parted and sent me a beige angel? Come here Southern Star. *Aaja*. Come come.

We are shooting a Bollywood blockbuster with the Ashok Patel.

It's called *Bindhi Beach: Bollywood to Bondi*! I'm India's number one director. And you, YOU must replace Patel while Patel's patella gets a replacement.

WERTHEIM

From *A Rabbit for Kim Jong-il*
by Kit Brookman

A Rabbit for Kim Jong-il *is the remarkably (preposterously) true story of a German rabbit breeder, whose giant rabbit Felix caught the eye of Kim Jong-il.Wertheim sold Felix to North Korea and rather belatedly tried to rescue him, with the help of Sofie, his local pet shop owner. They get caught and are put in jail. In this scene he has learnt that his execution could be quite imminent. The tone of what has, until now, being a mostly farcical play has shifted to become very dark, very quickly.*

I've been so stupid. I should never have taken that phone call. I should never have agreed to see Mr Chung. I was just flattered that someone was interested in my rabbits. I was flattered.

I had thought, with the rabbits, that I could create something… if not perfect, then beautiful, at least. I thought that was something worth striving for. But the truth is, Sofie, that the rabbits had become a routine. I don't know why I kept caring for them. I kept telling myself all the reasons, but time made the reasons sound hollow. I would wake up in the morning and tell myself that I was enthusiastic. Oh, another day I get to be with my rabbits, how lucky I must be that I get to spend my life in this way, how many people must dream of this, I told myself, spending all their waking hours in the company of the things they love.

Only I didn't love them anymore. They bored me. I reached the limits of my knowledge but had no-one to teach me more, and no-one was interested in sharing what I had managed to come up with. But I persisted, and my persistence in the face of hopelessness disgusted me, what a stupid fucker I must be, I thought. I hated myself for my pride in my work. What work? They were just a bunch of stupid rabbits.

I had loved them with all my heart but had no-one who would share that love. And like most things that can't be shared, that can't move, like most things that begin to pool in dark places, my love began to fester. I began to hate the rabbits for making me poor and ridiculous and alone because I had poured everything into them and no-one else gave a fuck.

So I stopped feeding them.

Who cares, let them die, I thought. Only I will know, and then they will all be dead and I can't begin again and it will all be over.

The first day they were confused, but not too distressed. As time went on, they got very thin. They began to bleat constantly. Their cries at night were horrible to listen to. I was killing them. I was killing any desire that I might have to go into that barn ever again.

After a little while I stopped hearing them. Oh, Sofie, I thought I had done it. I thought it was over at last and finally I could imagine a life without them, a small, easy life with nothing so distressing as hope ever appearing on the horizon.

And then the phone rang. It was Mr Chung with an enquiry about the rabbits. He hardly needed to say two words and I was running out to the barn to check on them, praying that it was not too late. The slightest hint of interest and I was reeled back in. Utterly, utterly pulled back in.

Maybe it would have been better if it had been too late.

How cruel it is to hope. How impossible not to.

JASMINDER

From *Melbourne Talam*

by Rashma N. Kalsie

Jasminder is a 17-year-old Indian Sikh living in a studio flat in Melbourne with two other people. His clothes hang on his frail body and his turban looks too big for his boyish face. In this scene he is talking to Mohit. Mohit is his flatmate and has gotten drunk, vomited in the shared bathroom and not cleaned it up. Jasminder is having a hard day. This monologue is intended for an Indian performer.

Can you feel the heat … do you think my fever's over a hundred and two?

He takes out a strip of medicine from his jacket.

I have the medicine for fever but it's past expiry date, do you think I can still have it?

He tries to show Mohit the medicine. Mohit does not look at the medicine, slips under the blanket.

Tu so—just go back to sleep … *Saala* useless fellow. Let me have it anyway. I have to leave in four hours for work, I need rest before I can start again. Studies *and the newspaper wallah* job is killing me …

He swallows the medicine. Switches off the light, sits on a chair.

This chair's so much better than my bed. I had picked my mattress off the street. Ranbeer allows only slim mattresses in the flat. My mattress is perfect for the room, but it is sagging now—maybe it's the moisture in the air. If I put it out in the sun it just might come back to its original shape. Sleeping on the floor is not a problem—I am used to it. Sarabjit uncle, my father's younger brother, used to come down from London to attend the weddings of our relatives. Uncle and his family were given the cots, whereas we slept on the floor. *Bebe*, my mother would say:

[*As mother*] *They are our guests, Jassi—they are not used to hardships.*

So I thought life is *easier* abroad. Sarabjit uncle had run away from home after fighting with my grandfather. Nobody knew where he was for ten years and then suddenly he returned with a suitcase full of gifts.

He brings his blanket onto the chair.

Sarabjit uncle is the hero of our family. He has seen the whole world and he drives a BMW. Uncle owns a big business in London, but there have been all sorts of rumours about him—someone from our village had seen Sarabjit uncle at Heathrow airport. He claims uncle was cleaning toilets! I don't believe him—people are jealous of Sarabjit uncle's success. How can a janitor buy a BMW? Bauji, my father, retired as the head postmaster of Gurdaspur, but he can't afford a BMW. He drives a scooter. Bauji could have bought a small car if he didn't have to pay my fees. We were hoping the money we got from selling our farm would pay for the entire course, but I've run out of it in eighteen months. Fourth semester fees are due in five weeks.

Biji, my grandmother, imagines my grandfather's spirit lives in our Gurdaspur house. Grandfather had built the house with his own hands. His ancestral house in Pakistan had been burnt down during India's partition. He lost everything—his parents and little brother were burnt alive with the house—but grandfather did not break down. He was a true Sikh, a fearless lion like we Sikhs are. He crossed the Pakistan border, lived in refugee camps and finally settled down in Gurdaspur. Our family has a strange destiny—we've been migrating for three generations, making new homes in new lands. This is my home now—this corner in a rented flat. Ranbeer found this flat for us. It was my second day at uni—I was looking for the library when Ranbeer walked up to me and solved all my problems.

Ranbeer became a housemate and an elder brother to me. We are all hard-up here—we go through hardships in the hope that we'll come out of it like Sarabjit uncle and grandfather. Whenever I feel bogged down I remind myself we are Sikhs—the warriors who fight to the end.

CONNOR

From *The Violent Outburst That Drew Me To You*

by Finegan Kruckemeyer

Connor is 16 and has some serious anger issues. His parents drop him into the woods where he is to stay, on his own, for a week to calm down a little. But then he meets Lotte, who is camping with her family. She's 16 and angry too. And they fall in love. This scene is just before they have to say goodbye—a rare moment of tenderness for them both.

And the plan starts …

It starts with you stealing your principal's car again.

Yeah. And you fill the tank—and then you come and pick me up.

It's night, and I stand there waiting, under a thin awning, with the rain falling lightly. A stray dog comes and he sniffs at my heels. He isn't scared of me, though, and that pleases me more than I expect.

Eventually the car pulls up, and when I jump in the passenger seat, you have a coffee held out already, and the smell of it warms me even before I put it to my lips. As we drive out of my street, you tell me a joke you just heard at the petrol station, and I laugh a little bit, but really I'm staring out the back window watching the dog as it sits there in the rain. It doesn't go under the shelter and it doesn't run off either. It just stands there and waits for morning maybe. I don't know.

We drive all through the night, and you never let me share the load. You say I just have to tell jokes and find radio stations and point out things we'll tell our kids about in years to come, when we're describing this drive and what it meant. 'What does it mean?' I ask you, and you laugh. 'That's a good joke,' you say. 'More like that.'

There's this one moment, maybe about four in the morning, when we drive right along the edge of a really high road and all the land below us looks purple and the cows sleep below us in the fields, even though I can't see them. And I imagine everyone asleep then, that I can't see, and us awake, and I say a little prayer for all of them (not a God prayer but a prayer prayer)—for every one of them with their knees up to their chest or a girl by their side or wrapped tight in their sheets or dreaming of being children again.

At sunrise we stop at a car yard and share sandwiches that I made, because I'm not a boy at all and do things like that. We kiss on the bonnet of a crumpled-up car, but then you wipe your mouth straight after, and I don't know if you have crumbs or if the kiss tasted wrong. And I don't ask either.

You say you'd like to learn to smoke right now, in a moment like this one, and I understand completely, because the sun is cold and it's so so quiet and the smoke would have done nice things in the sky.

After a bit, an old guy with an umbrella walks past us staring and we pocket our cling wrap, and get back in the car, and this time I'm doing the driving and you sleep on my shoulder. And I think this is maybe the happiest I've ever been, before or since—and if we just kept driving like this for the rest of my life I would have gone to heaven, no questions asked. And they would've recognised me there.

But as it is, you wake up an hour or so later and we stop at a town someway after that, and ditch the car, and get jobs and have kids and buy a dog, and live a long and happy life.

And now, I still think I'll go to heaven. But I don't know if they'll recognise me anymore, or if... if I just ended up looking like every other human.

NED KELLY

From *Kelly*

by Matthew Ryan

This poignant script is the imagining of Ned Kelly's last night before he faces the gallows. Dan, his brother, has arrived in Ned's cell, disguised as a priest. He is seeking Ned's forgiveness and blessing but the last time they saw each other (at the Siege of Glenrowan) Dan tried to kill Ned, a fact Ned finds difficult to forget. This script has many monologues, including Dan Kelly telling the other side of the story.

Do you have no knowledge of what I did that day? What I did for you? What the whole fucking country is still talking about?

I could have gone too, Dan. I could have got away and disappeared forever. But I looked back at the inn. That little house, surrounded by coppers. I thought of your stupid face, smiling. 'Of course he's coming for me', you'd be thinking. No question in your mind. Two dozen bullets in me, half my blood gone and ninety pounds of armour on. I could barely stand let alone walk. But off I went, closing in behind them. To save my baby brother. The first one sees me lurching out of the mist. They hadn't got a proper look at me in the dark. And here I was, this thing coming at them. Steam from the helmet, sunrise in their eyes. 'A headless monster', he screams. And didn't I look the part. He fires his gun, hits me, but I stay on my feet. Others see me, scared out of their wits. They had no idea what the fuck I was. They fire their guns and I fire back. One empties his gun at me and it doesn't slow me down one bit. Another shoots me in the face, breaking my nose against the helmet. And I congratulate him on it. 'It's the devil', they scream. And for a moment I wonder if they're right.

They fire rifles and shotguns but I push forward. Half the bullets going in but I'm too far gone to stop. More dead than alive, I was. I yell at you to come out and fight. Surely you will. I keep looking at the door, screaming your name. Smashing my gun against my helmet again and again, ringing it like a bell. Waiting for you to charge. But there's no sign of you. The coppers are on all sides of me now but I'm not stopping until I get to you. I'm not stopping. And then the strangest thing happens. Joe's horse comes up to save me. She just wanders up to me, ready to ride and take me away from it all. As if the ghost of Joe himself is on her, telling me to leave you there. But I don't. They shoot her twice and she falls. And then a bullet rips through my hand and I know this is it. This is my death. I scream at you to get out and I push forward, shooting at anyone I can, wanting every bullet in the place to head my way so you can get clear. And one of them gets in close behind me with a shotgun and takes me out at the knees. They rip the guns from my hands and the helmet from my head. And they realise who they've been fighting. I lie there pinned to the ground while the Victorian Police argue over whether to shoot me dead on the spot. One of them points his own gun at the other coppers and threatens to kill anyone who does me harm. At that point I was fairly certain I'd seen it all. And then you proved me wrong. I was the first to see you. Coming out the front door of the inn. No helmet on. Your rifle in your hands and the devil in your eye. I'd never seen such a look on your face. 'Jesus', I thought. 'The brave bastard is trying to rescue me.' And then you start shooting. But not at the coppers. No. At me. Screaming your lungs out. Firing again and again. The coppers have to drag me away to protect me from you. After everything I'd just done. A coward your whole life and it's me you try to kill.

GLEN

From *Michael Swordfish*
by Lachlan Philpott

Glen is 17 years old. He is quite matter-of-fact about some pretty serious stuff: his insecurities, his dead twin, his mother's grief. There is a dry self-deprecating humour running throughout, along with a strong dose of pragmatism. Although he reveals vulnerability throughout the monologue, at the end of the day he's happy to get his brother's TV in his room.

What's going on for me right now? Not much. Just you know, getting through school and shit. Shit, can I say that—shit I mean?

Cool.

School's okay. I don't love it or anything. Like if I got off the train and walked up the street and it had vanished one morning I wouldn't cry or anything. Yeah. Some guys would because it's their whole lives and everything. It can be like that, right.

The best things? The sport I guess. I do rowing. And cadets. I like cadets. I don't want to be in the army or anything like that. It's just about getting away. I like that you can get away in the bush and you don't get watched all the time, you get trusted not supervised and you have to survive and the discipline of surviving is what gets you through. I'm a CUO. My brother was one too. That's not the reason I wanted to be one. I don't have to do everything Seb does.

But it's like at school you get a certain amount of respect if you make it through and who doesn't want that? Respect.

Seb's two years older than me. He finished school last year, he's away on a gap year. Everyone always asks me where he is and I say Russia. I don't know if he's actually even going to Russia. Can you still go there? Mum writes posts to him and says hi or whatever for me. I don't have time to write right now.

I like that Seb's not at school now. It's not like we don't get on. It's just that Seb took up a lot of space 'cause he's really good at everything and I will never be as tall or as smart or as strong and …

I was a twin when I was born. Maybe that's why. Some people say I will always be a twin but my twin Lachlan was stillborn so he never got to see the world at all. There should have been four brothers. Seb, me, dead Lachlan and Ned. I never got to know if he would have been a Lach or Lachy or Lacho or …

If Lachlan had have lived we would have been a power block. Like: *Keep your hands off my twin or you die!*

I wonder what would have happened if Lachlan had have lived instead of me. Is that what makes me weak? Half of my life force got cut short and the joy of me arriving in the world was cut just after my cord. They'd bought a double pram and it's still in the back of the garage covered in dust and huntsmen's webs.

Mum always wanted a daughter. You can see it in her face sometimes. If any of us had been a girl they were going to call us Gay. We all dodged a bullet there.

There have been times when I thought Lachlan might just walk up the driveway and knock on the front door and say it was all a big prank and he's back now. That he'll be lying under the bed in my room waiting to jump out and scare the shit out of me. But instead there is just this space.

There are two living twins in the year below us.

The Leopard twins. Jack and Nick. They have spots. On their faces. They do everything together.

I wonder if Lachlan would have been like that with me.

Mum makes a fuss of my birthday to help cover up the sadness. And now Seb's gone. Which I know is totally different because he was like everywhere in my life—at school and at home—and Lachlan … When we saw Seb off at the airport he had a strange look on his face as he went through Customs and I said what would it be like if we never saw him again. Mum didn't find it very funny.

Mum's been standing in the door of Seb's room staring at his bed and Dad keeps saying: *Stop being morbid*. Went through Seb's things. I found some porn. All these DVDs and retro shit.

I have his big TV and shit all set up in my room now.

ROLAND

From *Toy Symphony*
by Michael Gow

Roland Henning is a playwright with writer's block. This scene (which, it should be said, is the first of many excellent monologues in the script) appears early in the play, when Roland is explaining the situation to his therapist. It's one of their first sessions. Roland is fiercely eloquent and very funny.

Okay, uh-huh. This is a technique, getting me to admit I have a problem, and then if I admit it then I have it. But I told you. I don't have writer's… block, there I said it.

And I mean writer's… thing, I mean it's such a meaningless term anyway, a Hollywood fiction, a monumental cliché and if that's how you're going to, if you think that's how you're going to whatever it is you intend doing or attempting, by removing this… block, as if, as if there's this there's this river, that comes bubbling up from the deep, way down in the Permian layers, thrusting up through the ancient strata, forced up by the internal forces, pressures, and it spills out, it bursts out into the dazzling light on the slopes of some painfully clear, bright mountainside and runs down this upper slope, this high country all clean and clear and sparkling like a Norsca ad, pure inspiration running over stones, through rapids, until it reaches the tree line. Then, there, it starts to wander through dank forests, spilling over mossy rocks and forming still, deep pools full of incredibly clear-sighted fish and visionary yabbies, carving out ravines all verdurous and gloomy with the slowly forming thoughts, just inklings of works of art. And then our river reaches the edge of the mountain ridge and now it plunges out of this high country, roaring over cliffs, cataracts, thundering over the edge of the falls, down into conscious valleys, deep chasms of impulse and first ideas, flowing on through steep gorges and wild, white water, churning up basic structures. It's violent and dangerous but finally it begins to slow down because it's reached the plains where there's habitation, creative cities full of neo-classical libraries and museums with all the previous works and commentaries and interpretations on show so they can be admired, where you can find inspiration and study whatever you need to build your own work. And after the city, it flows even more slowly so the happy peasants can draw the water from the river in their intricate, ancient watering devices to nourish the fields where the new works have been sown and where they start to grow. And then, at last, the river reaches the delta and splits into a dozen different tributaries and the mud is incredibly fertile and masterpieces spring up almost without anyone having to do any work and then our weary river winds safely out into the vast ocean, stately, grand, with loud Beethoven playing, out to where Leviathan lives, brooding at the bottom, sending up the simplest, grandest thoughts to keep the ocean busy. And then the sun draws up the water and fat clouds form, thundering with thought so basic it's before thought, chthonic thunderheads. And the clouds drift towards the mountains and get snagged and it rains and the water tumbles down through fissures deep into the earth and it all starts over again and again and again and suddenly. Across our river—bang. Warragamba Dam. And the flow is stopped. It's blocked. By a block, the river is blocked by whatever; impotence, fear of failure, fear of success, fear of death, whatever. And I struggle helplessly with that, until you come along, with the psycho-cavalry and you help me work it through until one day, through persistence and 'I will not be defeated' and 'I am a valuable person' and I don't know, the workings of grace, you fly in like dambusters and drop your bouncing therapeutic bomb and it explodes and the wall collapses and water pours out and floods the towns downstream, and everything gets washed away and cleared away and swept away and new levels of fertile mud are deposited and the river is flowing again. And. I'm saved. Now. If that's how you, if that's what I'm paying a hundred and forty dollars an hour for well… you know. I don't think…

He breaks down.

He snaps out of it.

I'm fine, I faked that, it's easy to do, been around actors long enough, so breaking down, the sobbing confession or the really sad moment in my past that's caused this isn't going to happen either, so there's no point… I won't be… okay? And don't expect me to imagine myself as a ten-year-old either, I'm not doing that, don't buy that for a minute, talk to my ten-year-old self, or relive teenage traumas so they lose their power, uh-uh, uh-uh. Is that all… all of that, you know, clear? It's not me, that's all. Not me.

MIKE

From *Ladies Day*

by Alana Valentine

Mike (aka Madame Ovary) is a beautiful young man who identifies as homosexual. He has been sent to a counsellor after being bashed and sexually assaulted at the Broome races. He is telling his story to Lorena, a playwright visiting Broome from Sydney. He is outrageous and funny and a great storyteller.

So they give me this counsellor and I immediately know we're not going to get along because what is she wearing?

Polyester.

And not designer polyester, though even putting those two words together is an oxymoron in my books, but this, ladies, is polyester, made in China.

I mean, I'm not being difficult, or sarcastic.

I'm deadly serious.

How am I supposed to listen to someone like that, let alone respect them?

It's forty-one degrees and she's in polyester.

And I've got mental health problems?

Friends.

So she asks me, 'What really makes you happy when you're really down?'

And I say, 'When I don't know what to choose, I choose a beautiful dress', and she laughs.

She actually laughs.

And then she says, 'Do you think your interest in dresses is a way of loathing yourself as a man?', and I say, 'Dresses are not bad for men. Air around the groin, delicate fabrics on the skin, discovery of the undiscovered waist—can all be new experiences for some men.'

And then she tells me that I should stop comparing myself to others and live my own dreams and that no-one is my enemy except myself.

No-one is my enemy except myself.

To a man who has been sexually assaulted.

I said, lady, my life changed the day I realised that I had been dressing down to please other people.

When I realised that the universe wanted me to enjoy luxury fabrics.

And you, sweetness, will get some pride when you *start* comparing yourself to others and take some interest in putting them to shame.

When you realise that other people's opinions do matter and that you cannot simply impress the pants off them but intimidate the hell out of them.

Happiness, my little polyester-swathed frump, is the day you realise life is about winning and losing and losing involves foundation that does not have a sunscreen component and winning, my pathetically dowdy little friend, involves a silk linen blazer with mother of pearl details.

Well, she burst into tears.

And so did I.

It was all very cathartic.

And then she told me that she'd become a counsellor because of her own struggles with self-esteem, that her mother had always criticised her weight and dressed her in loose clothing even as a child, so that she grew up with huge body image issues.

Poor petal.

And then she told me that her mother wouldn't even let her use tampons because she said it was going to take her virginity, so the poor woman was forced to use those hideous surfboard-like pads all her life, apparently until very recently.

And then she told me that that is really common among her Asian clients—don't go all weird on me, there are a lot of Asian Australians in Broome, okay, so she used the word 'Asian clients'—she told me that recently one of her Asian clients actually asked her not only how to insert a tampon but then asked her to actually show her, like go into the toilet and show her how she inserted it into herself. That, my darling, I said, that is real commitment to your work. And another client, if you can believe it, honestly thought that women urinated out of the same place that they menstruate.

And I said, 'Do you mean she's never put her hand down there to check?'

And we both howled with laughter.

She was crying with laughter.

And I don't have a vast knowledge of female anatomy, friends, but even I know that the urethra is separate from the vagina.

She was all pity and poor little uneducated mite and I was indignant.

Poor little mite my arse, I told her, get a mirror, put your hand down there.

Take a look while you're taking a piss.

What's wrong with you girls?

And what did you do with your entire childhood?

At this stage I began to accuse her of telling me fairytales.

No child doesn't take a good look and feel around, and no adult doesn't refresh that knowledge on a weekly basis.

She laughed again, and so did I.

So.

The session was an unlikely success, I'll tell you.

I felt much better afterwards.

She promised to go shopping before our next session and so did I.

She told me I was the most honest client she had ever had and I told her she was doing a really good job.

I thought I might stick around to help her out.

Shore up her self-esteem.

That sort of thing.

Honestly, there is so much work to do in this town, style-wise, you could devote a lifetime to it.

So much raw need.

It's just sheer charity to give back a little of what I know.

JORDAN

From *As Told By the Boys Who Fed Me Apples*
by R. Johns

Jordan is a soldier who has been classified as 'permanently unfit' and subsequently becomes a horse groom. In the monologue below, he is talking to Sandy, the only Australian war horse to return home from World War I. It is through Sandy that Jordan is able to establish an emotional connection, for the first time after the atrocities of war. The monologue begins with Jordan and Sandy on the boat.

It's you and me on the high seas.

He sways with the movement of the water. On the prow, looking out.

Those Germans can't hurt us.

Because home is calling.

Heading away from the whoosh of mortars.

You spooked by the roll of the waves?

Our mates down there with their glassy eyes. Watching the flying fish and whales play in the glassy sea above them.

Other mates trampled in pools of blood.

Peep goes the whistle and their broken bodies fall back on you, spurting blood, before they get over the top.

Whizzbang flash, lighting up the sky green and yellow.

Corpses crammed into trench walls that bloat and rot in mud.

Devouring our mates, spitting out arms and legs.

Screams and cries. Do they haunt you too?

It's so strange to feel free.

Just you and me in the salt air and the big black sky like the inside of a cow pissing out the Milky Way.

We'll gallop into the clouds, we'll gallop into the realms of all that will ever be, we'll gallop into a new life. You're my horse now.

The waves bringing us home.

The bells.

All the bells pealing across the bay, ringing for us.

We're *home*!

He is disorientated, watching the movement of men at the docks.

What do you mean?

I can't stay with the horse?

The war is over?

Where are all the horses?

Skinned and butchered?

Manes and tails to stuff furniture. Hooves for the glue factory?

Can't afford to bring 'em home?

But if the war's over, why can't I look after him?

So where's he going now?

Maribyrnong?

He's my mate.

We've been together all this time.

The boys in Palestine weren't going to leave their brave horses behind. Had to shoot them? Would have broke their hearts.

[*Angry*] Maybe they should have shot all of us!

He pulls out an apple.

I didn't want to leave you. Had to. It's the rules.

It was hard for me too.

Thought it would upset you, me coming and going.

Best to forget all that happened out there.

Start over.

Got the trams out. Then walked past the Maribyrnong River up here to the Remount Depot.

I had a feeling something was not right with you.

You've been all nervous.

Haven't you, mate?

In this dark place.

Neighing and pawing the ground with those hooves. I heard you.

I got it now too.

The war sickness in my lungs.

The cough and blood at night.

The sweats.

Dad dead. Have to look after Mum.

I've been dreaming of you at night …

Over there. Flemington. Where the river snakes, the grass brilliant green.

Melbourne Cup run there, best horses raced.

If all the horses of that race stood side by side, head to tail, till no more racetrack could be seen.

That's how many of you went, and in the end it was only one come back.

You. It's true.

So much sorrow in those thick and heavy eyes.

I'd set you free.

But you can't see no more.

You can't be free in everlasting darkness.

Those sweet patient eyes.

Blinded. Old blind horse.

It breaks my heart.

They want your head and hooves as mementoes of the war.

It was in the newspaper.

That head of yours will hang in a museum.

And the people will stare at you.

You've got a story to tell, all the stories you know.

Just remember all we shared out there

The truth we always told.

I promise you I'm going to dig your resting place.

It's against the rules they said. We can't pay you.

I don't want money, for the love of God. It broke my heart leaving him at the war's end. It's the least I can do now I'm here.

He'll be gentle as a lamb.

I'm a labourer.

I know how to dig. It's what I do best.

This is your place now.

That old stables on the top of the hill where you've dreamt

Your whinny in the wind that blows here.

I won't leave you here on the top of the hill, too cold.

When the wind blows in winter.

And you'll be forever looking out for me.

Better here on the side of the hill.

Closer to the dip where you can hear the river flow.

And the frogs croaking in the rushes of the swamp.

But your heart is here.

He touches his heart.

I'll carry it carefully.

They say racing horses buried on this land too.

But you ran the greatest race of all.

Today you're off on another adventure.

You know what to do when you hear that bullet.

You leap high.

And you'll look back and see your body lying there.

But your spirit is free.

As you head towards the sun.

RUBEN

From *Ruben Guthrie*
by Brendan Cowell

Ruben Guthrie is 29 and the Creative Director of an advertising agency. He is engaged to a Czech supermodel and Sydney is his oyster. He is also an alcoholic, a fact that he hasn't yet managed to grasp. The following is the opening monologue of the play and takes place at an AA meeting. There is a lot of cocky swagger to Ruben but you don't need to dig too deep to find the vulnerability.

Hello my name is Ruben Guthrie and I am…

Here!

In this lovely church hall, sitting in the circle—having a 'share'.

I um, as you can see—from my face and arm, I ahhh… had a bit if an incident. Accident.

He sings a line about accidents from 'You Can Call Me Al'.

Paul Simon peaked with Graceland, he peaked. And then…

Where were we? Group—yes my arm! Right we ahhh… had the Federation of Advertising Awards on Saturday night, at which I picked up the Gong for best ad and best ad campaign fourth year in a row just quietly—and so maybe I imbibed a little on the wing of my continuing success and decided to surprise everyone at the after party by jumping off the roof of the very tall hotel.

The ironic thing is I created the entire ad campaign: *How will you feel tomorrow?*

I um, I'm Creative Director of 'Subliminal'.

Which is basically an Advertising Agency, but we also Brand for companies/client, plus supply content and concept platforms for online and interactive media—our stuff is pretty raw, like say we do an ad for street wear we'll use real street kids not actors—shit like that. For me it's an ARTFORM—like lately I've been thinking Iraq you know, all those soldiers moving through civilian towns in their tanks, rolling over huts securing premises 'n' shit—and I think bam! Whack a Coke can in that scene; do you know what I mean? And come on—I mean let's face it, if you were a soldier in Iraq, and you'd just had a hard as fuck day controlling the chaos in that searing dry fifty-degree Iraqi heat, wouldn't you be stinging for a cold can?

Hot soldier rolls out of the situation, wipes the dust and shrapnel out of his hair… spots a machine, frosted over and fully stacked with rows of icy-cold black *love.*

I rest my case baby. Did someone say 'Truth in Advertising'?

And it *appals* me the way other agencies produce such manufactured, contrived like replicating, representations of, not, symbolically not representing… how life is—do you know what I mean?! Anyway. So my arm.

I look down over the guttering of the hotel roof; there must be a thousand Advertising types around the pool drinking and talking in black tie. I'm thinking this will go down in history as like, one of the coolest things ever to happen in the game—and you know, this kind of action is up to me, I am the designated renegade—so be my lease.

I took a hit from a little bag of Magic I had in my shirt pocket, knocked off the half bottle of Absolut Mandarin I snatched off Hot Waitress and crouched like Carl Lewis.

'Nothing can hurt you nothing can touch you. You're Ruben Guthrie.'

I'm running. And the edge comes quick and I'm out there!

I highly recommend it by the way; combination of 'caine, vodka, and *flight*—out with the eagles man, flapping my heavy wings and soaring I can fly—I'm flying—I can fly.

And I fucking judged it perfectly, landing smack bang in the middle of what I thought was a standard adult pool but soon discovered was actually a children's wading bath.

'Crack' was the noise that stopped the party. 'Lucky not to die' was the term they used in the hospital.

Didn't phase me—it's just a break it's all part of being a renegade you take the good with the bad and fuck… that's where people like me live, out on the edge man… and I try to explain that to *certain people,* but Mum and Zoya my fiancée here thought it was symbolic or something and that I should come to this place and admit…

Admit…

That I don't know the difference between a pool and a children's wading bath?

You guys must drink a lot of tea.

Is it compulsory to wear Kmart tracksuits or is it a coincidence that all of you are… wearing umm…

So look, I really appreciate you guys listening to me and everything and you all seem like a great bunch, I'd love to use you guys in something one day if I can find the right… *the right…*

But, ahh, yeah—I mean, after hearing your stories, like your tale Janelle about hiding in the roof of the bottle shop every night, and you Jeremy, oh and you Ken… Ken!!!! About drinking Jim Beam for breakfast then driving a forklift through your ex-wife's front window. I mean you guys—you guys need to lay off the sauce for shiz. I wouldn't be offering you guys a brandy chocolate if you were over my house.

Not even!

So yeah my name is Ruben Guthrie and I am in Advertising.

CYRANO

From *Cyrano de Bergerac*

by Damien Ryan

In Ryan's adaptation of Rostand's classic, Cyrano is a soldier, a swordsman, a poet, musician, fighter, philosopher and astronomer. Valvert, a theatre worker, has just called a spade a spade and described Cyrano's nose as 'very big'. Cyrano is disappointed with Valvert's lack of eloquence and is encouraging him to be more inventive in his description. We have cut some of the other characters' lines to create this monologue.

The things you could have said before this choir,
To belittle this eruption, this erection;
Oh, for a second chance, 'A muse of fire,
To ascend the brightest heaven of invention'.
Let me direct you; first, let's try—Aggressive:
'Fetch the guillotine! Let's amputate!'
No, too much attack, too early; try—Impressive:
'Wow! The blood bank must be thrilled when you donate'.
Theatrical: 'A plague on both these houses ...!'
Decorum: 'Please put that back in your trousers'.
Olympian: 'On'ya marks, get set— [*thrusting his head forward*] I never lose!'
Pythagoras: [*measuring his nose*] 'Bet the squares don't equal that hypotenuse!'
Erotic: Do you like 'nasal'? Just the tip!
Oh, come on, you've all seen a stiff upper lip!

Sightseeing: 'Ah, the pyramid of Giza—Jesus!—look at the pyramid on that geezer!'

A gift: 'For your coalmines … it's a canary'.

Aqualine: 'I'd love to see your Julius Caesar,

You could beware the Ides of March in February …'

Envious: 'Wish I could smoke in the rain!'

Bewilderment: 'You oughta see the grindstone …!'

Telegram for Mr Bergerac: 'Oh, again …

Paris wants to excavate more limestone'.

Friendly: 'Usher—I'd like to buy this man a drink,

A bloody Mary. No, a Looonnnggg Island ice tea.'

Curious perhaps: 'What makes you blink?

Is it reflex or too much gravity?'

Then just plain Thoughtless: 'You'd look good in mink.

But use your nasal hair, you'll save a fortune.'

Or—Controversial: 'I suppose you think

A face like this will legalise abortion?'

A huge reaction from the crowd at the scandalous reference, so he has to reign it back in to less offensive material.

Alright, apologies, apologies …

A touch more Gracious: 'You must be fond of birds,

To give them such a vast and Gothic perch'.

Existential, or if you like, Absurd:

'We've found God! He has a portable church'.

Artistic: 'Your self-portrait … is a landscape,

Isn't it?', or perhaps Geology:

'Is that a rock, a headland, or a cape?

Looks more like a *peninsula* to me!'

Cartography? Ohh yes: 'Hope that mountain's not to scale …!'

Moby Dick? You'd have me call my nose a whale? Well …

'We've found her, Cap'm, thar she blows'!

Archeological: 'We also found the Grail!
'It was there the whole time, right under his nose!'
Desperate: 'Give up smoking, you can do it,
We've lost a dozen chimney sweeps this week,
It's Dickensian to put these children through it;
Close those Satanic Mills, it's just too bleak'.
Or …
Captain's Log, 'We're four miles from the peak!'
Surgical: [*sniffing*] 'Ah, I think we've lost a nurse …'
Emily Bronte: 'There's some Heights to make you Wuther'.
Oedipal: 'This cold is like a curse,
Give me a tissue, wife'. 'What am I, ya mother?'
Commercial: 'A sign! … For a perfumery!'
Fiscal: 'Don't open both of those accounts'.
Biblical: 'When it bleeds, it's the Red Sea'.
Grateful: 'Well … I guess it's the snort that counts …'

He finds a newspaper on the piano.

Ah, the classifieds: 'Warehouse available! Subdivided!'
Déjà vu: 'I've seen that nose before … No, I can't pick it …

Beat.

I mean I really can't pick it!'
'Oh, I know you now … you're um … you're … Easter Island!'
Transport: 'On the Metro, do you buy two tickets?'
Typical actor: 'Bet the acoustics up there are fantastic'.
[*A sudden sneeze*] Aachoo!—'Hayfever! Get a beaver! We'll build a dam!'
Costume party: 'Okay, that mask is a little drastic …'
René Descartes: [*with a big sniff*] 'You stink, therefore I am …'
St Nicholas!—Easy one, come on … piece of cake …
'He sees you when you're sleeping, he NO … SE when you're awake!'
Anthropological: 'It's just a myth;
An illusion made with mirrors; it's a stunt,

National Geographic said it was
The Hippocampocamelelephunt'.
Postmodern: '… nose …'
Punctual: 'You're early! No … you're late!'
Botanical: 'Do you stop and scare the roses?
And how'd you grow that moustache in the shade?'
Wisdom: 'Have you ever heard the saying,
"Don't cut off your nose to spite your face?"
Well, some maxims are not worth the obeying,
Just cut it off! It's not spite in your case!'
Paranoid: 'Can you smell what I'm thinking?'
A Pun!: 'That tower is an eye-full … what a feat!'
Forecast: 'Either he sneezed or it's sprinkling'.
Romantic: 'That nose by any other name …
would smell as sweet'.
Shall I go on or have you got The Point?
I skipped Pastoral-Historical, but felt
That Tragical could never disappoint:
'O that this too too … solid flesh … would melt'.
That's the sort of thing you might have said,
Had you had even a modicum of wit
In that vacuous unlettered feathered head,
But … I'd never let you get away with it!
[*deeply personal now*] I carry my adornments on my soul.
Don't think I don't care how people see me.
I never leave the house until I'm sure
I smell of immaculate liberty,
And polished independence. No manicured hands,
But I give my scruples the once-over.
True though. I wear no gloves, you got me there,
I have this one, left over from a pair,

A pathetic war-torn glove is produced.

A lonely thing, its brother I can't trace,
I must have left it in some viscount's face.

He belts Valvert with it, viciously.

THE DOUBLE

From *Lake Disappointment* by Lachlan Philpott and Luke Mullins

This is the opening scene of the play. The Double is the body double of Kane, one of the world's biggest movie stars. The Double is on set for the art house film Lake Disappointment *and is standing in a lake. It becomes quickly apparent that the Double is a narcissist with little idea of his own insignificance. The following is his inner monologue.*

There was this girl in my year at school. Everyone called her The Rabbit. She twitched. Did this thing with her nose. What was her name?

Rebecca?

Rachel?

When she stopped being called——and started being called The Rabbit.

Ruby?

Ruth?

Rochelle? I can't even remember her face. Just …

Oh, look! A fish!

I went fishing once when I was a kid. Didn't catch anything, but the guy next to us kept pulling them in and grinning away, standing on their faces and ripping out the hooks. Then he cast his line the wrong way. The hook curled back into his face, kind of tore his nostril, so much blood. He probably has uneven nostrils now.

Looks cold and it is.

I'm standing in the lake but that's not all I'm doing.

People walking down here with their rods. Past the church and the diner and the row of houses, the big plastic fish with the sign in its mouth. Fucking fishing. Watch your faces. Come and eat my worm. Come and eat my worm. Oh, you ate the worm, I'll put another one on. Come and eat my worm.

This town's a bit weird.

But it's only five weeks. Five weeks. Thirty-five days. And then Paris. Easy. Paris.

Bonjour.

Je m'appelle.

Baguette.

Helicopter for the aerial shot. It'll actually be me you see in the film.

Rhonda? Rhoda? Rabbit ... rabbit. Dressed as a rabbit for the Easter bonnet parade. Rabbit who?

Kane'll be on set tomorrow. Looking forward to seeing him. Haven't seen him since we shot *Path of the Willing.* Got a picture in my mind how he'll be. His sixpack. The little mole on his neck. Can't wait to see how he's looking.

Kane has to beef up for the Paris role. We both do. They want us to be really big for the fight scenes—so more protein, less carbs. We both have a bit of work to do to get the look right—but I think I'm going to get there.

When we did the concentration camp; that was hard. Took him forever to get all the ribs to show. I beat him. Easy. He made a good Jew but I was better, even he said that. But we both made good Jews. I had to start eating more because I was too good.

He should've won the Oscar, should have been a shoo-in, but Michael played that autistic man. Shame 'cause he didn't have to physically change and they overlooked Kane. Again.

Kane's character, my character, our character in this film can't find the lake. He looks for it from the moment he drives down the mountain into town. He searches for it all day and night, stays at this guesthouse called The Lakeview, but he can't see it. He goes for a walk to find it but he can't, and all the time he's surrounded by people who have been waterskiing and fishing and paddling about.

There's a boy in a blue cap at the edge of the water watching me.

You get used to it.

He looks towards the boy and smiles.

Bonjour.

Back to us.

This is an independent feature. Low budget, high stakes.

Gina, my agent, says this could be Kane's crossover film, his potential McConaughey moment. This script. This director. It's awards material. There is a scene in this that Gina's excited about. It's going to see us doing some pretty breakthrough stuff.

Rita?

Ricky?

[*To his crew*] Okay.

He relaxes.

They had a class reunion. Wonder if Rabbit went? I didn't go. I should have sent my hands along. People would have recognised them. My hands are more successful than anyone else's entire body.

I checked online for a gym before I came, but the name of the town didn't even come up. No flights go here because there isn't an airport. Kane will probably helicopter in.

I drove. But it's all good—I like driving. Gave me time to plan for Paris—the diet, the workout routine.

[*To his crew*] Again? Okay.

He takes the pose.

I stopped at a gas station on the way and there was this guy there, didn't say a word, but as he filled the tank, I saw his hands. The way the sunlight hit his knuckles and made the grease sparkle. The strength of his squeeze on the pump.

He recognised me. He does that thing men do when they recognise me, keeps trying to look me in the eye. I pay cash instead of credit and say you can get a picture if you want. So he gets his selfie with Kane and I make his day.

I drove down the mountain into town, hit the main street, and then it got really dark. I couldn't see a thing. Just kept hearing this rumble. There must be a waterfall that flows into the lake.

When I finally found the place I'm staying, the light came on on the front porch and there was this little hobbit dwarf thing there. I didn't know what it was, and then its face screwed up and it reached out and shook my hand and said, 'You've arrived. I'm Linda. I'll show you to your room.'

Am I on the wrong set?

Renee?

Kane and me were both rising stars. I was rising to the top of the hand-modelling world and Kane was doing his plays.

Then there was *The Taxidermist*, our first film.

People still do that cat sound at me in the street. Kane didn't cope with the fur, but we clicked. The director said so. Everyone said so. And it's there on screen.

So I stopped hand modelling and after that he gave me this.

A wristwatch.

Do you like it? Kane did the ads.

The boy in the blue cap's still staring. Must be a *Taxidermist* fan. That's still our biggest film.

He's sure I'm him. Check this out.

[*To the boy*] 'Stuff this, motherfucka. Get out of the pool.'

Kids all love that line.

I'll give him an autograph later. Then I'll find a gym and send Kane a pixt.

Sound travels on water. You hear all sorts of random things out here.

Giggling.

Rumbling.

Silence.

Rowena!

MARTIN

From *The Spook*

by Melissa Reeves

Based on a true story, The Spook *follows ASIO mole Martin Porter in his attempts to infiltrate the South Bendigo branch of the Communist Party. At just 19, Martin is quite innocent of the ramifications of his actions and not very well trained for the surveillance he undertakes. The following is quite a long monologue, running over seven minutes, but you can cut to suit your needs. The monologue is set in Martin's bedroom. He has a brand new tape recorder on the desk in front of him, with a microphone on a stand. He presses record.*

Testing. Testing. This is … Iago.

Last night, the fourteenth of October, I attended a party at nineteen Brighton Avenue, East Bendigo, the home of Elena and George Tassakis. They appear to be Greek.

He pauses.

I arrived at the party at nineteen hundred hours. At that stage of the evening there were four people present. George Tassakis, Elena Tassakis, Chris Tassakis and Cally Tassakis. Wine was served. George Tassakis said he'd made it himself. He showed me a barrel in the shed. It was full of wine. He said he'd been making his own wine for seven years and this was the best yet. Chris Tassakis and Cally Tassakis were given wine to drink. They are eight and twelve years old.

He presses pause. He looks at his notes. He presses record.

Altogether twenty-seven people attended the party at Brighton Avenue. I succeeded in learning eleven names. George Tassakis. He's about fifty years old, short, with a round face, going bald. He has a fish-and-chip shop. Elena Tassakis, that's his wife, quite pretty…

He rewinds and replays to find the spot and wipes 'quite pretty'.

She's younger than her husband, with a slight build. Long black hair. She stayed in the kitchen for most of the night, until the dancing began. Chris Tassakis, their young son. Cally Tassakis, their daughter. Very precocious. She handed out little slogans reading—'Stop the Imperialist War'—and asked me if I was a communist. I told her you don't ask people questions like that. She said, in this house you do. In this house you nail your colours to the mast. By this she presumably meant the huge Soviet flag hanging on the chimney. She said, come into my bedroom and play cards with me. I said, why in your bedroom? She said, you'll understand if I tell you what sort of cards I want to play. I said, what sort of cards do you want to play? She said, strip poker. I said, where did you learn to play strip poker? She said, at the Eureka Youth Club. That's the communist youth club they've got here, like a sort of commie girl guides. I said, what else do you do at the Eureka Youth Club? She said they do Russian peasant dancing.

He consults his notes.

Jean Bennett, a lady about thirty years old, thin with mousy brown hair. She lives in Leichhardt Street, Bendigo, works in the library. Drank to excess. Raylene Bennett, her sister, a cosmetician. She left the party early, said she'd rather be at home listening to the radio. She tried to make her sister go with her but her sister wouldn't go. They fought quite loudly at the gate.

He consults his notes.

Manni Dimitriades, something like that. I'm reasonably sure he was a cousin to Georges Tassakis. Been in Australia three years. Got a very thick accent. Frank Nash, about fifty, bushy hair, strong wellbuilt sort of bloke. I've seen him round town. He works at the Railway Transit office in Currie Street. Wouldn't have picked him for a commie in a million years. And Phyllis, dunno her last name, missed it. Arrived with Frank Nash. They're definitely not married to each other, but they were… intimate, you know. She has reddish brown hair and a high-pitched laugh, like a horse, and she wore this lowcut green satin dress and high heels. She spent most of the night in the kitchen with Elena Tassakis. They both came out when the dancing began. She was mad with Frank Nash for not dancing with her, so later she danced on her own and made a spectacle of herself.

He switches off the record button. He takes out a packet of cigarettes he has hidden under the table. He is nervous and excited. He lights a cigarette, smokes half of it, blowing the smoke out the window. He butts it out and goes back to the tape recorder, consults his notes and presses record.

There's two more I got names for. Lance Whitney, middle-aged bloke, missing two fingers on his right hand… and Mick Leavis, the guy that sold me the *Tribune* in the pub. A big bloke with a beard, says he went to Russia when he was twenty-five as a merchant seaman, says it was like he saw a vision of heaven and he's been a communist ever since… Oh and there was Paul something or other, a dentist, left pretty early… I missed the rest. I didn't wanna write anything down, even in the dunny, you know, like you said, but anyway… What else…?

After supper everyone gathered in the backyard. George Tassakis introduced Frank Nash as the reddest red in Australia. Frank Nash made a speech thanking Elena and George and talked about the Soviet Union and China and said China was making it very difficult for the Soviets to send their weapons into North Vietnam. He said things were in a sorry state if China could forbid the Soviets to use their air-space and tell them to catch the train. He said that it's very damaging for international communism, and that someone called Sam Arnold had wanted to show his Chinese slides at this very get-together, but that Lance had told him to go and book the Town Hall and see how many turned up. Everyone laughed. Then he said, raise your glasses to the workers of the world and the Communist Party of the Soviet Union, and everybody cheered. Incredible, you know, the neighbours could hear all this stuff. Then people did these little performances. Mick Leavis did a poem, something about a man dying down a mine, and the cousin, Dimitriades, did a Greek dance to a record on the record-player that they brought out into the garden, he was pretty good, he was a bit of a hit with the ladies, and then Lance Whitney, the guy with the two fingers missing, he bloody well played the banjo while the lady that works in the library, Jean, did a hula dance in a grass skirt. Most people started leaving after that. There was a bit more singing and dancing and stuff, and they passed a hat around collecting money for a man in prison in Greece, someone called Glazzo. The stayers didn't finish up until o-two-thirty or so in the morning, with the men sitting around in the kitchen talking about the election, bagging Menzies, and the ladies washing the glasses, chiming in with stuff. The women seem just as deep in it as the men, couldn't believe it, the words that came out their mouths, it's like they've been brainwashed or something… I felt like I wasn't in Bendigo. I don't know where I was… but it was a right little nest of reds on Saturday night. After Frank Nash left they played cards for money. I lost seven shillings.

He pauses.

I was wondering if I get that back at all?

CREON

From *Antigone*

by Damien Ryan

In this adaptation of Sophocles' Antigone, *Ryan has transplanted the action from ancient Greece to a modern day war zone. As in the original, Creon is the King of Thebes and the following takes place on the first morning of peace. He is trying to usher in democracy after a brutal civil war. In the following he is addressing thousands of his people in the morning sun. He stands on a pile of shattered bricks.*

Good morning. I did a very unusual thing late last night, a lost ritual, I hope you all did something similar. Around a table, in my home—outside actually—on a clear night, I sat with my family … and we ate a meal. A *rationed* meal, before you point fingers.

There were no sirens, no incendiaries—for forty minutes not even a phone call. I didn't hear the screams of children playing, early days for that, but I didn't hear the screams of children dying either. Just … silence.

The flares and mortars of the Argyve army, the roar of their engines and artillery, the ruthless hearts they wrapped in vests and sent into our cafes and markets to kill us where we lived, those faces from our children's nightmares have turned in retreat.

He holds up a dossier.

This is the confirmation from Chief of Army. They're gone. It's over.

Applause and wild celebration from the people, which he cuts quickly down.

At a terrible cost. I can't lie to you, you can see it, we're devastated—our city, our infrastructure, agriculture, industry—the power grid.

But we didn't talk about war … at dinner, last night. Instead, we spoke about the stars, well my niece spoke about the stars, at some length, and we listened.

She bemoaned that so many of our Greek names for the stars are gone, replaced with the names of scientific instruments—there's the final frontier of our empire dispatched.

He gestures to a particular area of sky.

One in particular she showed us, a constellation called Arcas, one of Zeus' sons. I woke this morning still thinking about it. An arrogant king wanted to test Zeus to see if he was who he said he was—a god—so he invited him over, to dinner, and served Zeus his own son—to eat—his dismembered body. I struggled with my ration during this bit. The test being: can the father, at the critical moment—before he devours him—recognise his own son? Does he have to actually taste him to know who he is? Unfortunately—you can see where this is going—Zeus dined. When he realised his mistake …

Silence.

Well, it's lucky he's a god. He collected the parts of his son and made him whole again. Made him a constellation among the stars. Arcas.

A god has eaten our children too—I think this was my niece's message to me—a merciless god, the god of war. We fed them to him if the truth be told, as we always do with the young, the strongest, the bravest.

Very personal to the people around him, perhaps taking each by the hand.

I wish I had the power to make them whole again. Or at least to mark the night forever with their light. I can't. But I can help us learn from the *beauty* of their lives, and their sacrifice.

Our old gods taught us something about beauty, didn't they, something that made sense a millennia or two back. 'That which is beautiful is good.' Greece seemed to accept the definition, our artists conceived from it, our architects proved it in the grace of our buildings. Our mathematicians, philosophers, musicians—well, most of our musicians. That which achieves proportion, balance, measure, is beautiful.

His effortless, almost casual eloquence has become more formal now, building to something, a measured intensity.

The beauty I speak of this morning lies out on the plain, beyond our seventh gate. It is the body of a man, a boy really. His hip is open to the view, the bone splintered to a mosaic, his left hand missing above the wrist, his face cut clean through, like sugar loaf, and his blood pooled deep on the stone beneath him. His skin is already blackening in the heat, flies breed in his wounds. I gazed upon him through the long dawn. When you watch with patience you can actually see the sun move—the steady march of light revealed each cavity and shattered joint of the boy. And in the glare of day I saw true beauty. True goodness. He was my nephew, Polynikes. And his rotting body is the most beautiful thing I have ever seen.

A sudden change in Creon—a quickly accelerating severity.

It is in perfect harmony with his *crime*, perfect *proportion*, precise *balance*. He was a traitor, to his state, to his god, and to his family. He brought chaos and death to his own people, to his own brother—for there, in the same light, in the same blood, as once they were in the womb, lay Eteocles, his twin, slaughtered and slaughterer, dead in the same moment. But *his* blackening body was not beautiful. This was the hideous death of a hero. A practical death. He will feel our gentle breath, our tears, be given burial, libation and the full ceremonies of the fallen. Polynikes, his brother, who with this lawless militia, said, and I quote, he would 'Kill until the human soul could recognise no god'—he said this on a video while removing the head of a thirty-one-year-old woman who worked at the city library. I knew this woman. She use to press the returns, the paperbacks, with a warm iron so they looked unread for the next borrower, because, and I'll quote her too: 'A book should be like a child opening its eyes for the first time'. He, as I told his family last night, he is going to help us heal.

Now, I made you two promises in the final months of this conflict—that this day would come—and that when it did, we would sleep the sleep of a free people, and awake to find the age of kings dead. I have inherited a chair in that palace. Today we call it a throne, tomorrow just a chair, like any other. We'll put it in the courtyard, you can sit in it and feed the birds! Because tomorrow I join you as the servant of a new master—Democracy. Interim president of an open, multi-party, representative government—

Significant and growing applause, shock, raw emotion from his people.

Accountability, an end to sectarian violence and repressive censorship, real tolerance, real checks on executive authority, free elections, don't imagine it, see it, an economic development zone, investment, employment—Freedom. I'll say it again. Freedom. But understand, new democracies die like lambs. A reborn Thebes will have to play at miracles with time—we must age years in a day. In this day! With tomorrow's dawn, and the next, and the next, while its most vulnerable, our democracy has to open its young branches to the wind without losing its roots to the inevitable storm—because the sun is up today, but storms will come.

My nephew, Polynikes, lying in that sun on the Aonian Plain, is the carcass of a violent ideology—of fear and fundamentalism—and our carrion birds, Thebes' great eagles, the very symbols of our freedom, are already hard at work, picking apart that ideology. They will devour it, tear its flesh to a thousand fragments, carry it high on the winds, and deposit it where it may never again reassemble itself. His flesh gone, his bones will lie on that hot earth, untouched, unburied, unmourned and forgotten. Except by the dogs whose teeth perfect his beauty.

Your king for a day, this is my decree.

Bury him in our soil, anyone, we will unbury him and you will lie with him. Mourn him and you will join him.

Good morning, Thebes. It is a good morning. The sun is up. Let us work.

Silence. He steps down from the rubble to move away, but senses the uneasiness among his people.

You're the voice of this city, you're free to speak.

Beat.

Don't pity my family or my decision. My family is yours, each family is the state's.

Any city can rebuild—this boy's body, festering back to earth, is our moral soil, on it we rebuild our character.

YOUNG BOY

From *Suit*

by Christos Tsiolkas

In *Who's Afraid of the Working Class?*

by Andrew Bovell, Patricia Cornelius, Melissa Reeves and Christos Tsiolkas

First performed in the late nineties, Who's Afraid of the Working Class? *was born from Jeff Kennett's Victoria. This young boy is in his mid-teens and this is the opening monologue of the play.*

I love Jeff Kennett. I think he's a good guy, a sexy guy. I like it that he's tall, I like it that he's smart, I like it that he doesn't give a shit about anyone. He's an arsehole, I know that. He's a cunt. It's obvious. He's a silver-spoon-up-his-arse cunt, he can't hide that, but I don't care. He's not whingeing all the time, not bludging, not making excuses. He's got style; he looks good and he knows it; he's got class. It's written all over him. But, he's not soft. He's not soft at all.

Not like my dad. No, not at all like my dad. My old man is one of those guys who's wasted his whole fucking life. He works a shit job, has for thirty fucking years, since he was a kid, pouring concrete. And, man, you should listen to him, listen to him go on about it. 'I'm so tough, we brickies are so special.' Yeah, right. Hasn't done a fucking thing with his life. Hasn't seen the world, hasn't had an original thought. Nothing tough about him except his mouth and his forearms and even they're going to fat. My mum's no different. She's brain-dead as well.

My father hates Jeff Kennett, calls him scum, says he's destroying the unions and the working class. But I can tell that deep down inside he respects him. You've gotta. Kennett doesn't give a shit about anyone, does whatever he likes. He even stands up to that ugly piece of shit, Howard. And that's the leader of his fucking party! Kennett is a legend. Bet my old man wouldn't mind being like that, instead of following orders all his fucking life. Weak cunt! Just a day, just one day, I'd like to see my father be like Kennett. Just fucking once.

I want to go down on Kennett. When I do go down on a guy, when I come to that, it'll *have* to be someone like him. Tough. Arrogant. Knows what he wants. That's my favourite wank dream. I'm with school, an excursion to Parliament House. Somehow—I skip over this bit while I'm pulling off—Kennett and I end up in a lift. It's him and it's me. Sometimes there's this other guy, some suited, young, wog guy I saw on the Channel Nine News, some wog guy who hangs around Kennett. Sometimes he's there, banging away with us, sometimes he just watches. And then sometimes he's not there at all.

The lift stops. There's a moment that the light flicks off, then it flickers back on again. Kennett puts a hand on my shoulder. He's way tall, way taller than me. He notices I've got a stiffie in my school pants, I'm stretching the cotton. He's dressed real fine. Beautiful suit, slim tie. He winks at me and then it's on. Every time I wank to this, it changes. Sometimes he's hairy, blonde curls, all over his chest and stomach. Sometimes he's smooth. He doesn't take off his clothes, just opens his shirt, unzips the pants. I dream that his dick is squat and thick, and that when he comes, he comes in fucking buckets. Just pours the come over me, over the wog guy. That's my favourite wank.

Fuck! I could come now. Man, I could come all over this fucking stage.

I wish I could tell my father about this dream. Maybe that would get the cunt alive. Poofter son, father, you've got a poofter son who wants to fuck a real bloke like Kennett, not some boring working stiff like you. He'd crack, I know he'd crack it. How to tell his mates on the job? 'My son's a faggot.' Gutless cunt. He could never do that.

Kennett, when he got elected, there was this big rally in the city. It was fucking enormous, about a hundred and fifty thousand people. He had closed down my old high school, that fucking waste of space. It was nothing but a factory churning out dole casualties. They should've torched the place long ago. But Mum and Dad, of course, Mum and Dad were angry. [*Mimicking*] 'You got to come to the rally, it's important.'

So I had to go, with Mum and Dad. Dad kept bumping into all his scuzzy alco mates; even the young ones looked sick from their shitty useless jobs. I liked the crowd, it was exciting, I loved being there in all that mass. I thought we could do anything, fucking pull apart this shithole of a city if we wanted. I wanted it to get angrier, I wanted it to get bloody, like it happens on the news overseas. The cops were there, waiting. I wanted it to get bloody, so I could bash some cunt cop right in the middle of his fat, ugly face. I wanted to kill a cop, then go right off and torch fucking Chinatown. That would have been a fucking winner, man. Kill a cop and kill a gook. But it wasn't that kind of rally. It was [*contemptuously, in an effeminate accent*] *political*.

I managed to get up close, near Parliament steps, next to this really drugged-out feral chick and her dread-head, dead-head mates. I sat near the steps, bored now that the marching had stopped. Some union wanker was going on, whingeing about what everybody already knew. 'The government doesn't care about hospitals, Kennett doesn't care about education. This government sucks.' [*Shouting*] All governments suck, you brain-dead cunt!

I looked up. In the window there was Kennett, looking down. Some ponsey guys around him were nervous, shitting their pants because of the crowd. But not Kennett. Nah, not Kennett. You know what he was doing, you know what the cunt was doing? Kennett was laughing. He was watching us and he was laughing at us.

That moment, that's the moment I knew he was a God. That's the moment I thought you are one smart mother-fucker. All around me people were singing union songs. Crap hippie shit. We shall bloody overcome for Christsakes. I looked around, looked around, saw my old man. There he was, little Sammy Destanzo, little Sammy who hasn't done one thing of any note in his whole wasted fucking life. Little Sammy Destanzo who is forty-six and fucking looks sixty-eight. There's my old man, chanting along, doing the old nazi salute to Kennett who doesn't know who the fuck Sammy Destanzo is and who will never know who Sammy Destanzo is because Sammy Destanzo is a big, fat nothing.

I couldn't wait to leave this crowd of morons, these fucking sheep.

Dad says to me, do you want a job on a building site, and I just look at him. A real dirty look. He goes ape-shit, calls me a bludging cunt. I don't listen. He wants me to work on a building site, he wants me to be like him. I'd rather sell my body for twenty bucks in St Kilda, I'd rather be a fucking whore. Work, grog, sleep. Work, grog, sleep. Work, grog, sleep.

That's it, that's my old man. Three lousy little words.

I'd like to fuck Kennett. That would be the best. I reckon he's got a hairy arse and big red balls. I'd like to fucking ram it right up him. I'd like to do it again and again. That would be cunt worth fucking.

One day I'm out of here. I'm not going to be trapped in fucking Dandenong watching that dumb, plastic arsehole Ray Martin night after night. One day I'm going to have lots of money. I'll steal it, I'll beg for it. Fuck, to get out of here, I'd kill for it. I'll get style, I'll learn about the coolest places to be, I'll have all the best-looking guys hanging on me, begging to have a go at sucking my dick.

One day I'll be above Jeff Kennett. I'll be above all of you, you'll all be little specks, little nine-to-five, seven-to-three-thirty little earthworms.

Work. Till you drop.

Drink beer. Till you rot.

Sleep. That's the best part of your lives.

He spits on the stage.

I can't wait to vote.

He exits.

GABRIEL YORK

From *When the Rain Stops Falling* by Andrew Bovell

The following is set in Alice Springs in the year 2039. In this scene, Gabriel York, aged 50, is standing, holding a fish that has fallen from the sky. It's the opening scene. Like the rest of the play, it resounds with humanity, humour and hope.

I do not believe in God. I do not believe in miracles. I cannot explain this.

It began with a phone call. It was Friday evening. About ten pm. Which was unusual. The phone rarely rings and never at that hour. I was reading. As I do before bed. A history. *The Decline and Fall of the American Empire 1975–2015*. I am fascinated by the past. Which may, at least in part, explain the fish.

I have not seen a fish like this for many years. Not since I was a boy. I mean I have seen pictures of them but not one in the flesh. They are, after all, or at least they are meant to be, extinct.

Though I have heard rumours that they are still occasionally caught and served, secretly, in the most exclusive of restaurants, but only for the select few and only for those who can pay. If I was to purchase such a fish, if purchasing such a fish as this was still possible for the man in the street, it would cost me a year's wages. I could never dream of affording such a delicacy. If such a delicacy still existed.

He looks at the fish.

Which strangely, it seems to do.

He lays the fish on the table.

I hesitated before answering the phone. Wrong number, I thought. Surely. Who would call me? Me? At this hour?

It was my son. Andrew.

The name was his mother's choice. I had wanted to call him Joe. After a man I once knew. Joe was a good man. He told me he only swore once in his life and that was the day he met my mother. And he was always losing his hat. He liked to walk and one day he went for a walk and never came back so it was probably better that it was Andrew and not Joe.

I haven't seen Andrew for many years. I left when he was a boy. It was cowardly of me, I know. But I was not the fathering type and to be perfectly honest I thought the boy had a better chance without me. I sent money, of course. When I could. And a card. Now and then. For the first few years. I'm not proud of it.

Anyway there he was… this Andrew, this son of mine, on the phone at ten pm on a Friday night. 'Hello? Is this Gabriel York? It's Andrew here. Your son. I hope you don't mind me calling you like this. I hope you don't mind. It's just that I'm in Alice. And I was wondering if I could see you. Dad?' Only it went more like. 'Hello?… Is this… Gabriel York?… It's Andrew here… Your son… I hope you don't mind me calling you like this… I hope you don't mind… It's just that… I'm in Alice… And … I was wondering if I could see you?… … … … Dad?

And my mind was racing, trying to stay calm, trying to take each piece of information in and just as I came to terms with one extraordinary fact, such as 'It's Andrew', he would say something else, like 'Your son', until I felt unable to reply and the longer I said nothing the harder it became to say anything at all and so I hung up. And returned to my book. *The Decline and Fall of the American Empire… 1975–2015*.

I can't imagine what he thought of me.

I tried to concentrate on the page I was reading but found myself re-reading the same line over and over again, its meaning escaping me, when

I tasted something salty in the corner of my mouth and realised that I was crying. The tears were falling from my eyes, rolling across my cheeks and gathering in the corners of my mouth. And of course I knew I was crying because of him, hearing his voice, the voice of an adult now when I could only remember the child but it also felt like I was crying for so much more.

So I lifted the receiver and recalled the last number. 'Andrew?… I'm sorry. That was unforgivable of me.' And he didn't say anything and I realised that he was crying too and I wondered whether his tears tasted as bitter as mine. I hoped not… 'I'm so sorry,' I said… 'I'd like to see you very much. Why don't you come for lunch tomorrow?'

And as soon as I had given him my address and hung up I knew that it was a mistake. Lunch? What was I thinking? What would I give him? I can hardly feed myself let alone a son I haven't seen for what… twenty years? What do you serve for lunch in circumstances like that? I mean lunch hardly seems the point.

And besides what will he think of me? Me? I mean what will he think of the clothes I wear? My suit? Which looks alright from a distance but up close is quite shabby and old-fashioned. Second-hand. Or third perhaps. But certainly not purchased new. And my shoes, worn at the toes and down at the heel. And will he notice that I don't wear socks? Not if I don't sit down or cross my legs. If I remain standing my son won't know that I don't wear socks.

And what will he think of my room? It isn't much. It isn't anything at all. A one-room bed-sit on the twelfth floor. Not the kind of place a father should live. Surely. And it needs a paint and the carpets are worn. And it's dirty. To be perfectly honest, it's filthy. In the corners and on the window sills and the ceilings. Layers of dust and dirt and grime and dead insects. Years of neglect. And will he notice the smell? Of a man who lives alone. I mean I wash. Of course I wash. But not often. There hasn't been the need. Until now.

And so I began to clean it. The room. That night. A bucket of hot water and soap suds. I washed the walls, the ceilings, even the light fittings were scrubbed. I washed the door handles and the light switches and the dark corners behind the furniture. I scrubbed the table and the floor and polished the windows. I dusted the books and the lampshade and even took to the grouting between the tiles with a toothbrush. And by morning, when I had finally finished I looked around and it looked exactly the same. So I found an old tin of leftover paint in the cupboard. White. Or off-white. Pure white being too stark. Like a hospital. And I pulled the furniture to the centre of the room and covered it with sheets. I took the pictures off the walls. I took the books from the bookcases. And I painted. And I painted. And I painted. And when I finished I looked around and it still looked exactly the same. Only whiter.

And I began to feel angry. Why did he call? Why is he doing this? What does he want from me? Money? Is that it? Does he think I'm worth something? Does he think I owe him something? And as I'm thinking these thoughts I'm also thinking how terrible, how irrational, how baseless, how shameful it was to have these thoughts. How shameful I am. How appalling I am.

What kind of man am I?

And then I realised that it was Saturday. He would be here in an hour and there was nothing to eat. I wanted it to be special. I wanted to feed my son something substantial. Something nourishing. Something to make up for all those meals I failed to provide. And there was nothing in the cupboard. So I went out. And it was raining. Pouring. It has been for days. Still is. The river is swollen and threatening to break its banks. Two of the bridges have already been closed. And I didn't know whether I would make the shops or even what I would buy if I got there. And it was too much. I just couldn't manage it. I couldn't look after him then. And I still can't. I just can't. And I screamed. I just screamed. I opened my mouth and screamed and a fish fell out of the sky and landed at my feet.

And it still smelt of the sea.

I don't believe in God. I don't believe in miracles. I cannot begin to explain how a fish can fall from the sky in a town surrounded by desert. I cannot begin to explain this. But it is truly the most wonderful thing that has ever happened to me... And now all that is left for me to do is to put the fish in the oven and wait for the knock on the door.

I know why he is coming. My son. I know what he wants. He wants what all young men want from their fathers. He wants to know who he is. Where he comes from. Where he belongs. And for the life of me I don't know what I will tell him. For whilst I know a great deal about the decline and fall of the American Empire, my own past escapes me. All I have are a few fragments, a few bits and pieces I found in an old suitcase after my mother's death. I don't know what they mean. I don't know how to make sense of them. I stopped trying to years ago.

The past is a mystery.

He looks at the fish.

And yet, perhaps it will be easier to explain than the fish.

SOURCES

Bovell, A. (2009). *When the Rain Stops Falling*. Currency Press, pp. 1–5. Copyright © Andrew Bovell. Extract reprinted by permission of the author.

Bodie, J. (2011). *This Year's Ashes*. Currency Press, pp. 49–51. Copyright © Jane Bodie. Extract reprinted by permission of the author.

Brookman, K. (2016). *A Rabbit for Kim Jong-il*. Currency Press, pp. 44–45. Copyright © Kit Brookman. Extract reprinted by permission of the author.

Brown, N. & McCool, S. (2016). *Lighten Up*. Currency Press, pp. 12–13. Copyright © Nicholas Brown & Sam McCool. Extract reprinted by permission of the authors.

Conigrave, T. & Murphy, T. (2006). *Holding the Man*. Currency Press, p. 161. Copyright © Timothy Conigrave & Tommy Murphy. Extract reprinted by permission of the authors.

Cornelius, P. (2011). *Do Not Go Gentle…* Published in Cornelius, P., *Do Not Go Gentle… / The Berry Man*. Currency Press, pp. 45–46. Copyright © Patricia Cornelius. Extract reprinted by permission of the author.

Cornelius, P. (2011). *The Berry Man*. Published in Cornelius, P., *Do Not Go Gentle… / The Berry Man*. Currency Press, pp. 104–105. Copyright © Patricia Cornelius. Extract reprinted by permission of the author.

Cowell, B. (2011). *Ruben Guthrie*. Currency Press, pp. 1–3. Copyright © Brendan Cowell. Extract reprinted by permission of the author.

Flack, E. (2015). *Ivanov*. Currency Press, p. 9. Copyright © Eamon Flack. Extract reprinted by permission of the author.

Frankland, R. (2017). *Walking into the Bigness*. Currency Press, pp. 38–41. Copyright © Richard Frankland. Extract reprinted by permission of the author.

Gow, M. (2008). *Toy Symphony*. Currency Press, pp. 2–4. Copyright © Michael Gow. Extract reprinted by permission of the author.

Johns, R. (2017). *As Told by the Boys Who Fed Me Apples*. Currency Press, pp. 30–34. Copyright © R. Johns. Extract reprinted by permission of the author.

Kalsie, R. N. (2017). *Melbourne Talam*. Currency Press, pp. 12–15. Copyright © Rashma N. Kalsie. Extract reprinted by permission of the author.

Kruckemeyer, F. (2015). *The Violent Outburst That Drew Me To You*. Currency Press, pp. 35–36. Copyright © Finegan Kruckemeyer. Extract reprinted by permission of the author.

Miller, S. (2015). *Caress / Ache*. Currency Press, pp. 35–36. Copyright © Suzie Miller. Extract reprinted by permission of the author.

Mueller, R. (2016). *A Town Named War Boy*. Currency Press, pp. 45–46. Copyright © Ross Mueller. Extract reprinted by permission of the author.

Mullins, L. & Philpott, L. (2017). *Lake Disappointment*. Currency Press, pp. 1–4. Copyright © Lachlan Philpott and Luke Mullins. Extract reprinted by permission of the authors.

Mulvany, K. & Silvey, C. (2017). *Jasper Jones* (revised edition). Currency Press, pp. 1–3. Copyright © Kate Mulvany & Craig Silvey. Extract reprinted by permission of the authors.

Murray-Smith, J. (2014). *True Minds*. Currency Press, pp. 137–138. Copyright © Joanna Murray-Smith. Extract reprinted by permission of the author.

Philpott, L. (2017). *Michael Swordfish*. Currency Press, pp. 18–20. Copyright © Lachlan Philpott. Extract reprinted by permission of the author.

Purcell, L. (2017). *The Drover's Wife*. Currency Press, pp. 10–12. Copyright © Leah Purcell. Extract reprinted by permission of the author.

Reeves, M. (2005). *The Spook*. Currency Press, pp. 1–4. Copyright © Melissa Reeves. Extract reprinted by permission of the author.

Ryan, D. (2017). *Antigone*. Published in Ryan, D., *Antigone / Cyrano de Bergerac*. Currency Press, pp. 23–26. Copyright © Damien Ryan. Extract reprinted by permission of the author.

Ryan, D. (2017). *Cyrano de Bergerac*. Published in Ryan, D., *Antigone / Cyrano de Bergerac*. Currency Press, pp. 103–108. Copyright © Damien Ryan. Extract reprinted by permission of the author.

Ryan, M. (2013). *Kelly*. Currency Press, pp. 37–39. Copyright © Matthew Ryan. Extract reprinted by permission of the author.

Sewell, S. (2003). *Myth, Propaganda and Disaster in Nazi Germany and Contemporary America*. Currency Press, p. 86. Copyright © Stephen Sewell. Extract reprinted by permission of the author.

Thomson, K. (2004). *Wonderlands*. Currency Press, p. 15–16. Copyright © Katherine Thomson. Extract reprinted by permission of the author.

Tsiolkas, C. (2000). *Suit*. Published in Bovell, A., Cornelius, P., Reeves, M., Tsiolkas, C. & Vela, I., *Who's Afraid of the Working Class?*. Currency Press, pp. 1–3. Copyright © Christos Tsiolkas. Extract reprinted by permission of the author.

Valentine, A. (2016). *Ladies Day*. Currency Press, pp. 6–8. Copyright © Alana Valentine. Extract reprinted by permission of the author.

Whittet, M. (2015). *Seventeen*. Currency Press, pp. 28–29. Copyright © Matthew Whittet. Extract reprinted by permission of the author.

RELATED TITLES FROM CURRENCY PRESS

Not in the Script

John McCallum & Jenny Nicholls

This monologue collection offers up a challenge: to perform with voices that aren't from play scripts. Working instead from fiction, non-fiction and poetry, these pieces are a fresh and sharp source of material for performance, auditions and workshops. Unusual sources provide the actor or drama student with a new array of monologue possibilities.

The characters range from lovers in the *King James Bible* to a sci-fi Artificial Intelligence unit navigating gender identities between planets. Classic sources include *Great Expectations, Jane Eyre, Ulysses* and *The Bell Jar* and work from Beckett, Kafka and Mark Twain. Strong contemporary monologues come from work by Raymond Carver, Miranda July, Elena Ferrante, Jeffrey Eugenides, Alice Munro and David Sedaris. Australian voices speak in iconic moments from *Jasper Jones* and John Marsden's Tomorrow series and from definitive work by David Malouf, Elizabeth Jolley, Geraldine Brooks, Morris Gleitzman, Jeanine Leane, Gayle Kennedy and Alice Pung.

These monologues speak from moments of radical change and subtle exploration. Beneath each is a well-crafted literary work with its own world of characters, conflicts and tension: we invite you to look beyond the script.

978-1-92500-583-7, also available as a digital edition.

The Actor's Audition Manual

Dean Carey

The first edition of *The Actor's Audition Manual* quickly became known as the 'red audition bible', making it the essential guide. Now revised, it brings together a wealth of practical advice and a fresh range of speeches from Australian plays that will help make any audition powerful and effective. **NEW EDITION COMING MAY 2018 (print and digital).**